Steve Irwin

THIS IS A CARLTON BOOK

First published in the UK by Carlton Books Ltd 2006
20 Mortimer Street
London W1T 3JW

A CIP catalogue for this book is available from the British Library.

HB 10-digit ISBN: 1-84442-998-9
HB 13-digit ISBN: 978-1-84442-998-1
PB 10-digit ISBN: 0-14-300680-0
PB 13-digit ISBN: 978-0-14-300680-0

Editorial Manager: Lorna Russell
Picture Research: Paul Langan
Art Director: Lucy Coley
Design: Anna Pow and David Etherington
Production: Janette Burgin

Printed in Dubai

The publishers would like to thank the following sources for their kind permission to
reproduce the pictures in this book.

Alamy Images: /Don Vail: 18; **Camera Press**: /Chris Ashford: 75 **Corbis Images:**
/Theo Allofs: 10; /Australia Zoo/Reuters: 52; /Will Burgess/Reuters: 7, 126; /John
Conrad: 50; /Vera Devai/EPA: 120-121; /Najlah Feanny: 44t; /Michael & Patricia
Fogden: 12; /Eric & David Hosking: 104; /Tony Phillips/EPA: 62; /Lynda Richardson:
20; /Francis Specker: 74; /Greg White/Reuters: 9; **Empics:** 72; /AP Photos: 6, 38, 109;
/J. Cummings/All Action: 78, 79; /Russell McPhedran/AP: 39; /Lucy Nicholson/AP:
90; **Getty Images:** 56, 111, 117t, 118-119; /AFP: 115t; /Doug Benc: 114; /Heather
Faulkner/AFP: 115b; /Steve Holland/AFP: 113, 116, 123; /Bradley Kanaris: 112, 117b;
/Justin Sullivan: 77, 84; /Lisa Maree Williams: 42t, 42b, 43; /Kevin Winter: 8, 44b,
45; /Greg Wood/AFP: 30; /Jonathan Wood: 82; **Icon Images:** 11; **Newspix:** 36, 37,
47, 68b, 95l, 95r; /Jeff Camden: 100; /Channel 7: 14r, 16; /Courier Mail: 13, 19, 21b,
23, 25; /Marco Del Grande: 57; /Annette Dew: 88t; /Bruce Long: 97; /Rob MacColl:
124; /Lyndon Mechielsen: 98; /Graeme Parkes: 28, 29, 40, 49, 54, 59, 61, 64, 66,
68t, 69, 70, 71, 99; /Nathan Richter: 101; /Sharyn Rosewarne: 58; /Campbell Scott:
4-5, 34; /Megan Slade: 21t, 63t, 65; /Paul Trezise: 14l; /Adam Ward: 85; /Greg White:
3, 41t, 41b; **Photos 12:** /Collection Cinema: 80, 81, 88b, 89; **Retna Pictures Ltd:**
/Armando Gallo: 51; **Rex Features:** 22, 60, 94b; /Peter Barnes: 92, 93, 94t; /Miquel
Benitez: 110; /Peter Brooker: 67; /Stewart Cook: 106, 108; /MGM/Everett Collection:
76; /James D. Morgan: 86, 87, 105, 128; /Tess Peni: 63b; /Armando Pietrangeli: 103;
/United/Everett Collection: 83; /Wildtrack Media: 17, 24, 32-33; /Michael Williams: 26,
46, 53, 91

Every effort has been made to acknowledge correctly and contact the source and/
or copyright holder of each picture and Carlton Books Limited apologises for any
unintentional errors or omissions, which will be, corrected in future editions of this
book.

Steve Irwin

The Incredible Life
of the Crocodile Hunter

TREVOR BAKER

CARLTON
BOOKS

Contents

Introduction

Everybody in Australia, it's said, will remember where they were when they heard that Steve Irwin had died. Within hours of his tragic passing newscasters were already comparing the outpouring of grief to that experienced after the death of Princess Diana.

This reaction would surely have astonished Steve. Everybody remembered where they were when JFK was killed, but he was the president of the United States. And Princess Di, well, she was a princess. Steve Irwin was just a bloke who happened to love animals with an enthusiasm that came across well on TV.

So, in years to come, will people look back and wonder why the Australian Prime Minister John Howard took a break from the business of running the country

The 'modern-day Noah', as the CEO of the RSPCA Queensland described Steve Irwin, with his beloved animals.

to pay tribute to a TV naturalist? Or why the police had to enforce traffic restrictions around the Australia Zoo because so many people wanted to pay tribute to the work he'd done there?

It is not easy to say why his death had such an impact. The film star Russell Crowe said that 'he was the Australian many of us aspire to be', but even that doesn't quite do justice to the impact his passing has had. It's not just in Australia that the news of his death came as a terrible shock. In the USA and the UK there were similar reactions. Even Jay Leno in the States paid an emotional tribute to one of his most honest and entertaining guests, who had been on his programme more than ten times. Similarly in Britain, the BBC's website was bombarded with emails from people saying how much he meant to them.

Some tried to explain his appeal by saying that he was 'larger than life,' others that he was 'just an ordinary bloke' and, paradoxically, both claims seem to be true. He had an almost cartoonish energy that appealed to kids and adults alike, but he was also very approachable and down-to-earth – in the great Aussie tradition.

Nevertheless, the programmes he made for Animal Planet were very far from ordinary. They were unforgettable, unlike anything we'd ever seen. Before Steve came along the typical wildlife show was a hushed call to worship at the temple of nature. His programmes, in contrast, celebrated the excitement of getting down and dirty with wildlife at its wildest. People empathised with him because he understood that the natural response to catching sight of a 4-m (14-ft) croc is a flabbergasted 'crikey!'

On *The Jay Leno Show*, with Russell Crowe and host Leno. Both men made emotional tributes to Steve on his death.

People flooded to Australia Zoo to pay their respects to a much-loved icon.

Not everybody appreciated his style, of course. He wasn't a superhero and he probably made mistakes at times. The one criticism that must have hurt him the most, though, was that his actions were harmful to his beloved animals or to his family. Nobody could watch him on screen and not see his passion for the natural world or his love for his wife and children.

In this book we'll follow that passion from the early days at his parents' Reptile and Fauna Park to his incredible legacy of wildlife sanctuaries around the world. We'll see how an ordinary boy from Queensland became a TV star and then a movie star simply by being himself and doing the things that he loved.

By the time he died Steve Irwin was, for millions of people around the world, the number one symbol of Australia and not everybody was happy about that. With his khaki shorts and use of old-fashioned language like 'crikey!' they're probably right that he wasn't a very accurate representative of modern Australia.

Instead, he represented an idealised version of the country. According to one producer who worked with him in the UK he was 'the man the public would most love to have a beer with', which is ironic because Steve didn't drink. He wasn't the simple Aussie stereotype that some supporters and some detractors made him out to be. He was as complex, flawed and interesting as anybody else. An awful lot of people, not just in Australia, will remember where they were when they heard Steve Irwin had died, but this book is for people who want to remember how he lived.

The deadly Brown snake was an object of curiosity to the fearless seven-year-old Steve.

Chapter 1

The Early Years

Steve was just seven years old the first time his dad, Bob Irwin, noticed anything unusual about him. They were in the bush near his home in a suburb of Melbourne, where Bob sometimes caught snakes for the Commonwealth Serum Laboratory. Bob was a plumber by trade, but snakes were his passion and he was determined that Steve would grow up to share his fascination with nature.

Unfortunately, little Steve was perhaps too fearless. When his dad's back was turned he saw a 1.5-m (5-ft)-long Brown snake. This snake causes more fatalities in Australia than any other and they're the second most venomous snake in the

Schoolboy Steve, left.

Birthday gift. Steve was given a 3.5-m (12-ft) Scrub python called Fred for his sixth birthday.

Bob Irwin putting the finishing touches to the latest attraction at his Reptile and Fauna Park, a 10-m (33-ft) wooden crocodile, 1989.

world. Even at that tender age Steve should have known this but, before Bob could do anything, he'd got it pinned under his foot.

'I'm wearing plastic sandals, no socks either,' he remembered in an interview with ABC's Andrew Denton years later, 'And here's this Brown snake with its head on my leg and I've got it pinned, almost as thick as my dad's wrist. And he's gone, "whack!" and belted me out of the way, crushed me like a bug. I thought I'd come out of this a hero, but he thought he saved my life, and, you know, for months, he's scratching his head. "How come that kid never got killed by that Brown snake?" And I guess he figured it out then. He's figured, "This kid's got something."' What Steve had was a natural affinity for reptiles and a fearlessness that would eventually prove his downfall.

In retrospect, though, it's easy to say that he had no choice but to become a conservationist. A love for animals was in his blood. One of the things that first attracted Bob to Steve's mother Lyn was their mutual love for nature. Although Lyn trained as a maternity nurse and Bob was a highly successful plumber both of them dreamed of turning their passion into a vocation. They married when he was just 20 and she was 18 and critters of all kinds would be a huge part of their life throughout their long partnership.

To begin with, it was just an odd hobby, but gradually it grew in importance. Bob eventually pioneered new ways of capturing snakes and reptiles and Lyn made it her mission to rescue the many joey kangaroos, koalas, wombats and platypus that were either orphaned or injured by cars on the roads near their home. Even before they became full-time conservationists their home was always a haven for animals. 'There were [animals] everywhere,' Steve's childhood friend Tony Piscitelli remembered in a *Herald Sun* interview. 'Steve had an old pool out in the backyard. He had taken all the water out of it and filled it with sand and had reptiles living in there. Dad thought he was always a little crazy. He was, I suppose.'

Where other kids might ask for an action doll for their sixth birthday Steve knew exactly what he wanted, and he got it: a 3.5-m (12-ft)-long Scrub python! He wasn't allowed to play with it, of course. His parents were only too aware that the massive snake might have regarded young Steve as a nice meal. Still, he got to feed it and not from a tin of dog food, either. Like many kids, Steve and Tony used to spend a lot of time exploring at the nearby Moonee Ponds Creek.

'We used to spend hours down there catching carp by hand. There used to be frogs' eggs down there, too, and we used to bring them home and hatch them,' Tony said. But Steve's main interest was always in finding a nice snack for his python, now named Fred.

It was in 1970 that the path of his later career was really set in stone. Bob and Lyn made the decision to move the whole family, Steve and his two sisters Joy and Mandy, to Beerwah on the Sunshine Coast in Queensland, where they founded a new kind of zoo: The Beerwah Reptile Park. 'All varieties of Australian Reptiles in a safe, natural habitat,' it promised for just 50 cents for adults and 15 cents for children.

Steve, front right, with his friends from Essendon State Primary School.

Family snap of Steve with a big catch.

In 1970 even the more cuddly zoos weren't particularly fashionable. A zoo specialising in cold-blooded, resolutely uncuddly critters, must have seemed like a crazy idea. As Steve recounted to Andrew Denton, 'At that stage, snakes were something you hit with a stick, you know, crocodiles were just evil, ugly monsters that killed people and koalas and kangaroos made, you know, great, um, fur coats.'

It took them six months just to get the zoo ready for its opening day and for the first few years it was incredibly hard work. Bob had to fish and grow strawberries and peppers just to support the family. Meanwhile, Lyn filled the new house with even more animals.

'In my house, when I was growing up,' Steve continued, 'Mum would have 12, uh, pouches, you know, make-believe kangaroo pouches set up on the backs of chairs, virtually everywhere. So we'd have 12 little joeys, ranging from little pinkies all the way up to one year olds.'

It wasn't called the Reptile Park for nothing, though. 'Every wall that was spare had snakes in it,' Steve remembered. Where other kids might have been terrified Steve learnt to respect the snakes, even the deadly venomous ones. He later claimed that he'd handled more venomous snakes than anybody else in the world, but that he'd never been bitten.

This was because, from an early age, he learned that they will generally only bite if they're frightened. He worked out that, rather than grabbing a snake tightly around the back of the neck, as most snake handlers did, the best way to control them was to pick them up gently.

In fact, it's probably not strictly true to say that he 'worked out' how to deal with them. Steve was around snakes and other reptiles from such an early age that his response to them was almost instinctive. 'I've been playing with snakes since before I could walk,' he said once. 'It doesn't matter where or what it is, from the biggest to the most venomous.'

Later, some people would find his hands-on approach to wildlife shocking, but it was also the foundation of his celebrity. However, it was not to be snakes that he would be most closely associated with. Years later, when asked what his favourite animal was, Steve had no hesitation. 'Crocodiles,' he replied. 'They're living dinosaurs!'

The Early Years: Timeline

22nd February 1962 Stephen Robert Irwin is born near Melbourne, son of Bob and Lyn Irwin.

22nd February 1968 Steve receives a 3.5-m (12-ft)-long Scrub Python for his sixth birthday. He names it Fred.

1970 His whole family relocates to Northern Queensland where Bob and Lyn open the Beerwah Reptile Park.

1971 He helps capture his first crocodile at the age of nine.

1980s Like his father he volunteers for Queensland's East Coast Crocodile Management Programme.

1987 The Park has so many crocodiles that they open a separate Crocodile Environmental Park to display them to the public.

1991 He takes over management of the Park, which is renamed The Australia Zoo.

Steve with a baby crocodile.

Chapter 2

The Crocodile Hunter

In the 70s, the idea that anyone could be fond of crocodiles seemed completely absurd: people were terrified of them. They still are, but, as Australian suburbia expanded into what had been their territory, there was only ever going to be one winner. The hunting that went on was threatening to drive the fierce reptiles into extinction.

A colony of freshwater crocodiles.

The venemous Red-Bellied snake. Steve's school-bus driver hadn't expected to find seven of them in his cooler.

By then, Robert Irwin was considered an expert in the capture of crocodiles. He was asked by the Queensland National Parks and Wildlife Service to catch and relocate a colony of freshwater crocodiles. Their waterhole was about to be filled in and they had nowhere else to go. Although not as dangerous as the so-called 'salties' they still have powerful jaws, but, nevertheless, he decided to take his young son with him.

They set out in a small aluminium dinghy, armed only with a spotlight, and, to begin with, Steve mesmerised the crocodiles with the torch while his father leaped onto their backs and wrestled them into the boat. Eventually, Bob decided that Steve was old enough to bring in a little 'Freshie' on his own.

In his 2002 book *The Crocodile Hunter* Steve describes his first experience of wrestling with a croc after his father caught it in the spotlight.

'My fingers clamped around the croc's thick neck,' he recounts, 'My chin slammed into its bony head, my chest landed on its back and my legs wrapped around the base of the tail. I was being thrashed around in the muddy water. I saw pulses of light as I was being rolled over and over. I sensed the strength and warmth of my dad's arm feeling for my body. Whoosh! The next thing, both croc and I were slammed into the floor of the boat: "Are you all right?" Yeah, I got him, Dad." I saw his face in the beam. He was shaking his head in disbelief with a grin from ear to ear. That was start of my croc-jumping career.'

And this, apparently, was when Steve was just nine years old! During his early teens he would regularly accompany his father on croc-spotting trips. By then he couldn't wait to graduate from high school and follow his vocation. Even while he was still studying, he tried to help out at the Reptile Park, catching deadly snakes to add to their collection and occasionally terrifying even his snake-savvy father. On one memorable occasion he caught seven venomous Red-Bellied snakes and stored them in his school bus driver's cooler, much to the driver's disgust!

As soon as he could he started helping out full time at the rapidly expanding zoo. In 1986 he went away travelling for 18 months, writing to his parents 'every day' he said later, but when he came back he made the decision to move away, into the swamps of North Queensland.

Like his father before him he began catching rogue crocs, which had got a little to close to local communities. While the actor Paul Hogan was making croc hunting famous worldwide in the film *Crocodile Dundee*, Steve was living the life for real. He spent months with just his dog, Chilli, for company, capturing crocodiles with a net trap.

'I was totally feral,' he said later. 'I could run a wild pig down.'

He spent several years living on his own by the rivers of North Queensland, patiently waiting for big crocs to come by. He didn't even get paid for his services. The only payment he required was that he was able to bring all the crocodiles back to what

Eye to eye. Steve at work in the Reptile and Fauna Park, 1989.

A crocodile poses no threat to an adult hippo. The only hippo meat crocodiles eat would be carrion.

had now been renamed the Queensland Reptile and Fauna Park.

He didn't catch the crocs the easy way, either. Other crocodile hunters would often to sedate the animals once they had got them into the boat, but Steve refused to do this. He knew that there was a risk that the sedative could prove too powerful and actually kill the animal before he managed to get it home. He also insisted on using a soft-mesh trap, which could be dangerous, as it gave the croc a chance to spin around, but which was much gentler on the animal.

Absurdly, perhaps, he often seemed to put the crocodile's welfare above his own. At times it seemed as if getting great TV footage was more important than his own safety, too.

'One time,' he remembered in an interview, 'I crawled on my belly onto a sandbar in the middle of the Luangwa River in Africa and waited a few feet away from a hippo carcass for some crocodiles to appear and feed. Within a few hours, I was surrounded by more than 100 thrashing crocodiles fighting over the food. Any one of them could have changed their focus from the hippo and taken me out in a second.'

All of the 100 or so crocodiles that you can now see at the, once again renamed, Australia Zoo were either captured by Bob or Steve or are the descendents of those relocated crocs. Long before he was ever a celebrity

Off duty. Steve, in his early twenties, at Caloundra playing football with locals

Steve Irwin was regarded as a phenomenon in croc circles because of the number of successful catches he made.

He was so successful that some of Bob Irwin's friends weren't sure whether to believe that one man could do all that on his own. In response, Bob bought a video camera for his son. 'I had to get the croc into the boat, then from the boat to my truck, then into a crate,' he said in an interview with the *Sydney Morning Herald*. 'No one could believe that one person could do that, so Dad sent me up this video camera.'

From then on Steve tried, where possible, to film his exploits, tying the camera to a tree or propping it up

On duty. A 25-year-old Steve posing with Alister the Alligator.

ABOVE: Alister the Alligator, getting more sociable.

LEFT: Crocodile-feeding displays started in the Reptile Park in the late 80s, and became a hugely popular attraction.

on the seat of the boat. Although he didn't know it at the time this was the beginning of his TV career.

As time went by, Steve had more and more influence over what went on at the Reptile Park and it gradually expanded. In the early 80s it doubled in size when Bob and Lyn purchased another 1.5 hectares (4 acres) and in 1987 they had so many crocodiles that they were able to open the Crocodile Environmental Park. They could then arrange the displays of crocodile feeding that became the foundation of the zoo's increasing popularity.

In 1991 the Irwins had such confidence in their son's abilities that they felt able to retire and leave the park entirely in his hands, but he always gave Bob and Lyn all the credit for his development. 'Every time I'd make mistakes, they'd [say] "hang in there, lad, hang in there",' he told Andrew Denton. 'They just kept

helping me and persuading me to follow my passion, which was wildlife. And that, in essence, helped me be who I am.'

This, though, was only the beginning of his story. It is ironic that Steve became known as 'The Crocodile Hunter' when he was implacably opposed to hunting any kind of wild animal. 'Every chance I get,' he told one interviewer, 'I will put my life on the line to save crocs.'

'There are 23 species,' he said on another occasion. 'Seventeen of those species are rare or endangered. They're on the way out, no matter what anyone does or says, you know.'

Although he had no formal qualifications he probably knew as much about crocodiles as anybody. For obvious reasons the great reptiles hadn't actually been observed all that closely by scientists.

There are around 15 species of goanna native to Australia. This is a Gould's goanna.

'They're hard to study because if you go underwater with them they'll kill you,' Steve said. 'So we're catching them and releasing them fitted with telemetry gear to learn how they live. Many croc-related fatalities could have been avoided if we'd had more knowledge.' He called this project 'Crocs In Space' because it involved following the crocodiles' movements from space via satellite.

This meant they could work out how close the crocodiles got to built-up areas and see whether they really were a threat to people. Using this technology they were able to see that one crocodile, named Bananahead, successfully found his way home in just four weeks after they relocated him 52 km (32 miles) from where they'd caught him.

Steve even designed and built his own boat, the *Croc 1*, in order to have the perfect vessel for crocodile research. Despite his showmanship this attitude was always at the heart of his relationship with the animals. He wanted to know more about them for their sake and for ours. In 1985 when a new species of goanna (a kind of large lizard) was discovered in the rainforests

Steve with a friendly python.

of Queensland Steve immediately decided that he wanted to help with the scientific study of them.

He drove up to the Cape York Peninsula in his black and yellow four-wheel drive ('Old Yella' as he called it) and spent almost two months living in the jungle studying the behaviour of goannas and Green pythons.

After Steve's death Dr Leo Smith of the American Museum of Natural History in Manhattan said that, although Steve had no scientific degree, 'he could be considered a biologist rather than just a television personality. He was knowledgeable and seemed to care passionately about wildlife.'

'If you can't get wilds into people's hearts,' Steve once said, 'then we haven't got a hope in heck of saving them – because people don't want to save something they don't know.'

For all that he loved his crocs, though, Steve was honest enough to admit that the crocs didn't always love him. Years after he hunted his first crocodile he admitted to *Scientific American* magazine that one of his biggest beasts, a massive black croc called Acco, had a real problem with him. 'He hates me,' Steve explained. 'He hates me because I caught him out of the bush. Everyone for 20 years tried to kill him, so I went out there and I caught him. What a shame to pull the king out of his domain... Anyway, I cried long and hard at my camp when I caught that croc. It was just so disappointing that I had to catch him out of his bush. I did it because otherwise he'd be dead.'

It had taken Steve over 18 months of patient bush craft to catch Acco and he had a huge amount of respect for his adversary. It hurt him to see the former king sad and in captivity. Typically, he had an unorthodox way to deal with the problem. 'My job is to try and get him back on track where he's like, "Yeah, I am the biggest, toughest thing in here",' Steve continued. 'I'm feeble compared to him, and he just needs to see my ugly head again and go, "Yeah, I hate you," and push me out of his territory.'

Although he made his name capturing crocodiles it was always a last resort for Steve. He much preferred to see them in their natural territory. He even pioneered a way of helping them to fit in around people. In 1994 he was asked to do something about a large 'Salty' that was scaring people at 'Old Faithful Waterhole'.

In *The Crocodile Hunter* he says that 'Old Faithful', as the croc was christened, was merely being inquisitive. 'I guess when a large crocodile head, looking like a dinosaur, pops up near your camp or boat, it's quite intimidating,' he says with uncharacteristic understatement. Nevertheless, he didn't have much sympathy for this wimpy behaviour!

'What a shame!' he continued. 'I do not understand why park visitors were complaining about him, looking at people crashing around in your territory is hardly nuisance behaviour.'

Ingeniously, Steve captured 'Old Faithful' and then harassed him by loudly running the outboard motor of his boat and then firing several rounds from his gun into the water nearby. He didn't like having to irritate the croc this way but he knew that if it didn't learn to fear humans then it would probably be killed.

Despite his seemingly blasé attitude he always had respect for the awesome power of the crocodile – and the scars to show for it.

'When they strike it can be so quick that if they're within range, you're dead,' he told *Scientific American*. 'His head weighs more than my body so it's WHACK! It's that powerful. So fear helps me from making mistakes, but I make a lot of mistakes... I've been recently filming a 3-m (9.5-ft) female crocodile I had to catch,' he continued. 'Oh, man, she bit me up! That was a mistake.'

It wasn't just deadly crocodiles he captured. He used to relish heading into Australia's so-called 'Wild West' – the deserts of Central Australia – to capture the world's most venomous snake, the Western Taipan – also known as the Fierce snake.

When he'd become world famous, he was also sought after to catch the crocodiles' American cousin, the alligator. Steve had tooth marks on his arm from one encounter with a 'gator, but he was still happy to help when he heard about another one called 'Reggie' that was living in Lake Machado on the outskirts of Los Angeles. When he was small Reggie had been kept as a pet by a local man, but when he got too big to handle he was illegally released into the lake, where he fed on ducks, fish

Steve handling the world's most venomous snake, the Western Taipan, also known as the Fierce snake.

and other creatures. Ten different wildlife wranglers had tried to capture him without success before they called in Steve.

He immediately asked the local authorities to bait a trap with chicken and promised to return if Reggie made an appearance. Unfortunately, there was no sign of him and Steve suggested that it was quite possible Reggie had died in the murky water. 'The water is freezing and polluted,' he said, 'so Reggie may have died, or maybe he's dug a burrow and is waiting for his chance to surface. Wouldn't that be great!'

Perhaps his proudest and most exceptional wildlife encounter, though, was with a turtle. In the

early 80s, when he was first learning the croc trade, he saw the turtle splashing through the water. With its white head and pink nose it didn't look like any other turtle he'd ever seen or that was known to science. He tried to capture it, but it got away. Years later, though, he saw another one and this time he managed to capture it and bring one home. It was discovered to be an entirely new species and in Steve's honour the authorities named it *Elseya Irwini*, otherwise known as the Irwin Turtle.

Generally, Steve was always confident that he knew how to deal with any animals that he encountered. Even when he went to Africa and encountered lions for the first time he felt that he was in control of the situation.

'Within a half an hour, I'm going, "Wait a minute. These lions don't see me as a food source. They see me as a threat",' he said. 'So I mentioned this to the crew and we all stood up and went "Rah!" and the lions ran away. It was easy for me to work it out, I guess because of my instincts.'

The only creature he never felt comfortable with, bizarrely, was the parrot.

'I have a deep-seated respect for parrots,' he once said. 'As gifted as I am with all other wildlife, parrots have this uncanny desire to kill me. I'm not sure why, but they're like my kryptonite!'

ABOVE: A saltwater crocodile, and over page, freshwater crocs.

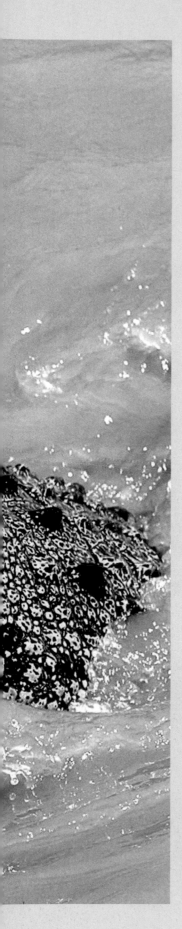

Crocodiles

The crocodiles that Steve first encountered as a child weren't the terrifying monsters of legend. They were freshwater or Johnston Crocodiles, which are much smaller than saltwater crocodiles.

Freshwater crocs can grow to be up to 3 m (10 ft) long, but that takes 30 years and most of them are much smaller than that. They're only found in northern Australia, mostly in lakes, swamps and the upstream areas of smaller rivers. They don't have a problem with salty water, but they do have a problem with the more aggressive saltwater crocodiles so they're never found in the tidal parts of rivers where saltwater crocs are found.

Ironically, if you're in a river where you can see freshwater crocodiles you may be safer than if you couldn't see anything at all. If there are lots of them around then their probably aren't any 'salties'.

When Bob was sent out to relocate them it wasn't because they posed a threat to humans, but because humans posed a threat to them. There are estimated to be about 100,000 freshwater crocodiles in Australia, and they are a protected species.

Nevertheless, if they feel threatened they can attack and they have razor-sharp teeth that can inflict serious damage.

Saltwater crocodiles, like Acco, totally deserve their fierce reputation. Unlike the slender, long-snouted freshwaters, they have a heavy, blunt head and even more powerful jaws. They are by far the most dangerous creature in Australia, relatively common across the north of the Outback, and they kill on average one or two people a year. They are the largest reptile in the world, up to 7 m (23 ft) in length and, in some cases, weighing over a ton. Their jaws can exert a pressure of several tons.

However, even they are far more at risk from humans than humans are from them. It takes females at least ten years to reach maturity and males 16 years or more. Even then only one per cent of the hatchlings ever reach that age and size. This meant that, when people began hunting them for their hides, their numbers collapsed. It wasn't until naturalists like Steve Irwin started defending them that they began to recover. Their numbers have now reached a level where some people have suggested that trophy hunting could be allowed again, but it goes without saying Steve Irwin was vehemently against that.

'We should be proud of our crocodiles,' he said in his autobiography. 'Here in Australia we don't have large predatory mammals, such as lions, tigers or bears; no, we're in the land of the reptile. The crocodiles are ancient animals dating back 65 million years. Today, virtually unchanged, they are modern-day dinosaurs.'

Chapter 3

Zoo Keeper/ TV Star

In 1990, Steve must have already felt that he was living the dream. The zoo was increasingly successful, he and his father had saved dozens of crocodiles, and their conservation work was increasingly acclaimed. Then, in the space of a year, he had two chance encounters that would change his life.

The first was with the TV producer and director John Stainton. John was already a successful filmmaker who had made many TV commercials and produced and managed shows with the famous Australian TV presenter Jackie MacDonald. Steve knew John because he had often used animals from the Reptile Park in his commercials.

One day, when John came to film another commercial there, Steve decided to hand him the stack of VHS cassettes that he'd shot on the camera that his dad had bought him. John couldn't believe his eyes. He ended up watching hours of footage without a break. He didn't know that it was even possible to wrestle crocodiles as Steve did.

They decided to make a one-off documentary together, but before they could Steve had another chance encounter that would also change his life.

In 1991, the year that he took over management of the zoo, Steve was performing his daily demonstration with a 4-m (13-ft)-long saltwater croc named Agro. Watching him was another wildlife fanatic, Terri Raines. She was a Canadian who ran the Cougar Country Rehabilitation Park in Oregon, USA.

'I'd been in the bush for two years catching crocs. Hadn't seen any Sheilas,' Steve remembered to Andrew Denton, 'And I'm doing a croc demo, and I look into the crowd and I see her and I'm like "Oh!". She stayed back and started talking to me and that was it – head over heels in love.'

TV producer and director, John Stainton.

Terri was only supposed to be taking a holiday in Australia, but when she spoke to Steve they found that they had a huge amount in common. They were both the children of passionate conservationists and both of them were committed to defending animals that other people were too scared to go near. From the start they were both smitten.

'Instead of showing how cool he was,' Terri remembered, 'Like, "Look at me, I've got a croc", he was wanting people to look at the crocodiles, showing them as passionate lovers and wonderful mothers.'

She asked him if he had a girlfriend, he said he did and whistled for his Staffordshire Bull Terrier Sui. This was only partly said in jest. According to Steve, Sui was incredibly jealous of Terri to begin with. 'Sui would sit in the front of my 4WD and wouldn't let her in,' he claimed. 'Sometimes she'd refuse to even look at her.'

Despite Sui's misgivings Steve asked Terri out to dinner and he was characteristically impressed by the energetic way she dived into a seafood platter. 'I'd never seen a girl eat with such gusto,' he told friends.

'We just totally hit it off,' said Terri. 'We had so much in common with the wildlife work, our passion and our goals, we had this great weekend and he put me up at the Glasshouse Mountains Motel. He was very chivalrous.'

They exchanged numbers and she went home to Oregon, but shortly afterwards he called her and said he was coming to visit.

'I never called him,' she remembered in an interview with *Sea Salt* magazine, 'and a month later he called, and this Australian voice came over the phone "G'day – I just want to let you know I can't stand it. I'm coming over in November – I will be there in two weeks and I am staying for 10 days."'

Eight months later the couple were married in Terri's hometown of Eugene, Oregon. When asked what his scariest moment was, Steve always said that it was when he got married! In his interview with Andrew Denton he still remembered the effect fear had on his marital relations.

'I was panicked, mate. I was so panicked,' he told Denton, laughing. 'I couldn't consummate the marriage, mate! I was freaked!'

'When we married, we'd spent less than six weeks together, and I couldn't understand what he was saying!' Terri told *Scientific American.* 'But I found Steve's passion for wildlife and willingness to lay his life on the line so exciting. What you have in our academic arena is a lot of people who are brilliant at what they do – and boring as the day is long.'

After spending less than six weeks together, Steve and Terri knew they were meant for each other.

They'd planned to have a normal honeymoon like anybody else, but while they were still in Oregon they got a phone call saying that there was a crocodile in need of help back in North Queensland. They dropped everything and immediately flew home. This time, though, John Stainton followed them as they went in search of the croc.

Unfortunately, the trip didn't start well. They discovered that somebody had got to the crocodile first and shot him dead. There was talk of going home, but Steve pointed out that if the big croc was dead there would still be other members of his family in the area and they would be endangered, too. For the first time Terri and John were to experience Steve's unique way of dealing with crocodiles.

He didn't go easy on them, either. Terri played a full part in every capture and on one trip had the terrifying experience of falling into a river where they'd left bait for a big croc less than an hour previously. 'I tried to stop thinking, but my horrible imagination wouldn't shut off,' she said in *The Crocodile Hunter*. 'I waited for the sensation of teeth piercing my flesh. I knew the crocodile would first grab my leg and that, with the kind of pressure its jaws exerted, my leg would be crushed. I would have no hope of escape.'

Steve should have been able to scare off any crocs in the vicinity by gunning the outboard motor on his boat, but at first it wouldn't start. Luckily he managed to get it going by giving the motor a good, hard punch and the film crew were able to haul Terri back into the boat.

In many ways it was exactly the same as any other croc-hunting trip Steve had ever been on, except this time he had Terri helping him and John's crew filming him. The results delighted everybody. John took the film to his friend Mike Lattin at Australia's Channel Ten, who was equally impressed. Later, when they

The *Crocodile Hunter* is launched on the viewing public.

Steve and Terri hold a 3-m (9-ft) female alligator, at Australia Zoo.

Open wide. The consumate professional, Terri shows no sign of distress.

aired it, the Australian public reacted in exactly the same way. It was a big rating success.

Despite the very public nature of their honeymoon, Steve and Terri did manage to escape the film crew occasionally, even when they were supposed to be working.

'We had a faster boat!' he laughed.

'We were in the mangroves with a four-person film crew,' said Terri in the *Sydney Morning Herald*, 'so it was hard to get any privacy. We'd [escape] up some tributary in the dinghy, and go, "This is romantic, but let's hope the boat doesn't tip over because there's a crocodile right there"… Believe me, I had mosquito bites where no mosquito has gone before!'

The first *Crocodile Hunter* was unlike any other nature programme on TV because of Steve's unique personality. All John Stainton did was to capture him being himself. Nevertheless, both Steve and Terri always gave the director credit for the way he managed to do that.

'A John Stainton production is real,' Terri told *Scientific American*. 'It is not a rubber crocodile. It is a guy who is out in the bush and he goes, "I think there is a koala around here that needs help." And he'll find a baby koala 18 m (60 ft) up a telephone pole somewhere.'

What was supposed to be a one-off documentary eventually became a series and John Stainton became Steve's manager. Over the next three years, ten more one-hour episodes were made. Their ultimate aim was to make the viewer feel as though they were right there beside him as he got closer and closer to wildlife.

'We've evolved from sitting back on our tripods and shooting wildlife films like they have been shot historically,' Steve told *Scientific American*. 'So, now it's not just, "Oh look, there's a cheetah making a kill." I want to take you to the cheetah. I want to get in there as close as I can to that cheetah. You'll see me in Namibia getting attacked by a female cheetah,

All in a day's work – filming *The Crocodile Hunter.*

Viewers had never seen anything like this before, and the show was an instant hit.

Although a TV star by now, Steve was committed to the family zoo, where this photograph was taken in 1996.

Visitors gather round to watch Australia's most famous, and most fearless, zoo keeper.

With a faithful friend, much-loved Sui.

Steve and Irvine the alligator embrace at the Central Park Boathouse, New York, 1995.

Steve on *The Tonight Show* with Jay Leno, wrapping an anaconda snake around his host.

Steve appeared on the show 14 times, accompanied here by two baby white tigers.

because I didn't know she had cubs, but the cameras are right there in a four-wheel-drive, filming me. She's "grrraagh!" putting mock charges on, and you get that overwhelming sensation that you're there, that you're with me.'

However, despite all of this they always believed that the main purpose of the programmes was educational.

'Our aim is to continue producing more wildlife programmes to entertain and enlighten,' Steve announced on the *Crocodile Hunter* website. 'We'll take the audience to some of the wildest and remotest

territories in the world. The time has come when all of us must be accountable. We don't own the planet Earth, we belong to it. And we must share it with our wildlife.'

'Our job in this world,' he continued, 'is to bring misunderstood and feared animals (as well as the cute and cuddlies) right into your house, so that we can share and learn about the world's wildlife.'

The Irwins were always proud that people who watched their shows would have a better idea of what to do if a loved one was bitten by a snake, or if they found themselves in croc territory. This well of knowledge was exploited by the producers of the reality TV show *Survivor*. When they filmed in Australia they got Steve to explain some of the dangers they might face with the snakes, spiders and other dangerous animals where they were filming.

But despite his new innovative style, Steve had a huge amount of respect for the old-school wildlife programmes.

'The natural history programmes made here are the best in the world,' he told the BBC's website. 'You've got the best film crews in the remotest

Steve with a Western Taipan snake (the world's deadliest), demonstrating how to control it with gentle handling.

countries living on fresh air and a little bit of water every now and again, catching some sensational wildlife pictures. And Sir David Attenborough, mate, he's like the Voice of God.'

Australian audiences, though, are notoriously hard to impress and it wasn't until Steve appeared on American TV that he was really regarded as a global star. Once again, this was thanks to Terri. After making

Steve had an extraordinary ability to relate to all animals, not just crocs and snakes.

The real Crocodile Dundee, feeding Graham.

the original honeymoon documentary she was visiting her parents in the US when she decided to show the programme to producers at the Discovery Channel.

Maureen Smith, the executive she met, wasn't impressed at first, Terri told *Sea Salt* magazine. Terri told Maureen that the film had done really well in Australia, but Maureen said, 'The problem is that here wildlife documentaries are 80 per cent animals and 20 per cent presenters. This is not documentary style, it's 80 per cent Steve in it, and 20 per cent just animals. It will never work.'

Terri told them, 'I know what everyone says, but if you just try it, it will be phenomenal... What is so appealing to Australians will be twice as appealing to Americans, because we don't have all this stuff.'

They wouldn't give her an answer right then so she flew home to Australia. A few days later she found out that they'd been given the go-ahead on a new channel called Animal Planet. At this time Animal Planet only had 200,000 paying subscribers. A year later they had increased that to 7 million. By the time Steve died that number had rocketed to over 70 million, most of whom, the network said, signed on for *The Crocodile Hunter*.

She was right. Americans took to Steve Irwin even more enthusiastically than his fellow Australians had. His path had been paved by Crocodile Dundee, but they couldn't believe that a real-life version actually existed. His extraordinary charisma also meant that he became a fixture on many chat shows, particularly that of the famous Jay Leno. Steve appeared on Jay's *Tonight Show* 14 times, memorably bringing alligators and venomous snakes into his studio, as well as many other animals.

These appearances also revealed another, underrated side of his character – a sharp wit and earthy sense of humour. Once, when Leno asked Irwin how he determined the sex of a crocodile, Irwin replied: 'I put my finger in here and if it smiles, it's a girl. If it bites me, it's a boy!'

'I've never met anyone who had such an enthusiasm for life,' Jay said after Steve's death. 'He was probably the greatest ambassador Australia ever had.'

Five years after the first *Crocodile Hunter* documentary was screened in the US Steve Irwin was reaching an estimated TV audience of 500 million people in more than 120 countries. By then, of course, his TV career had gone well beyond the crocodiles that had made his name. The final *Crocodile Hunter* programme was a three-hour epic that followed him around the world, visiting exotic locations like the Himalayas, China, Borneo and the Kruger National Park in South Africa.

Terri, who always went with him, continued to be amazed at his ability to relate to widely diverse animals all over the world.

'I've seen him walking with orang-utans after having never experienced something like that before,' she recalled to *Scientific American*. 'The mother comes down with her tiny baby – a little bald thing with the hair sticking out like a chicken – brings the little baby down and falls in love with him. The little baby orang-utan was up to his armpits up Steve's shorts and it made him squeal. That was the funniest thing.'

And, of course, he boasted throughout his life that he'd never been bitten by a venomous snake despite the many, many times he'd handled them.

'The Masai were amazed when I handled a Red cobra that spits blinding venom in its prey's eye,' Steve

A Red cobra.

remembered in one interview. 'I got squirted and had to wash it out with water – that turned out to be cow's urine. I dunno what was worse, the poison or the piss!'

Throughout this time, even though Steve and Terri were often away travelling the world filming, the zoo continued to thrive. In 2000 they bought another 28 hectares (70 acres) of land. In 2001 the City Council approved plans for a further $40 million upgrade. Between 2000 and 2002 visitor numbers increased from 200,000 to 600,000.

From being a small, family-run business it now employed around 500 people and in 2002 it won the Queensland Tourism industry award for the best major tourist attraction. At the time of his death Steve was estimated to be earning US $4 million dollars from the zoo alone. Most of this, and the even larger sums he earned from his TV work, were ploughed back into conservation.

Part of the credit for the success of the zoo has to go to Steve's best mate Wes Mannion. Although he grew up in Malaysia, where his father was stationed with the Royal Australian Air Force, Wes had a similar upbringing to Steve. There was dense jungle surrounding his family home so from a very early age he came in close contact with snakes and other reptiles.

In 1985 his family returned to Australia and at the age of 15 he made his first visit to Australia Zoo where he met Steve Irwin. When he saw what went on at the zoo he immediately knew what he wanted to do with his life and in 1988 he started working there full time. In 1995 he became manager of the zoo and eventually director.

From its origins as a small reptile park the zoo had just grown and grown and, although it is still best known for its crocodiles (thanks to Steve) they have gradually brought in more attractions. Most recently, Wes and Steve created the 'Tiger Temple', which allowed underwater viewing of swimming tigers and cheetahs.

Unexpectedly, though, their most famous resident turned out to be a Galapagos tortoise named Harriet. Everybody knew that she must have been incredibly old to have reached her impressive size of over 181 kg (400 lb), but in 2005 new research suggested that she might have been captured on the Galapagos Islands by Charles

Steve and Terri, with Wes Mannion.

Darwin in 1835. This would make her the oldest documented giant land tortoise in the world. Whether or not she was actually a key player in *The Origin of Species*, the famous book Darwin wrote after investigating the islands' wildlife was never exactly clear.

Some scientists argued that she was merely brought to Australia for her meat and, somehow, got lucky. However, tests revealed that she was indeed over 170 and, ironically, she'd been mistaken for a male

for at least the first 124 years of her life! Before being called Harriet she had been known as 'Harry'. Sadly, Harriet died quietly in 2006 at the impressive age of, it's believed, 176.

By then Steve had reached the point where every new TV series on Animal Planet brought in more visitors and his profile was still growing. With one new series, *New Breed Vets,* he even went well outside of his usual field, travelling the world searching for the most unusual and dramatic new

Harriet, the Galapagos tortoise, was believed to have been collected by Charles Darwin in 1935.

Steve places his hand in the jaws of one the world's most powerful predators.

techniques in animal welfare. It must have seemed a pretty tame project compared with his croc-wrestling days, but helped by Terri and John's business acumen, Steve Irwin had become a global brand.

Nevertheless, however famous he got he still took a very keen hands-on role at the zoo. This was

Graham the crododile's teeth marks in Wes Mannion's leg.

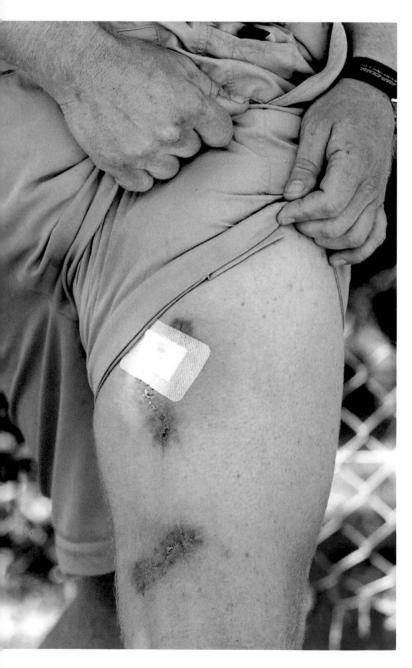

revealed to the world in shocking fashion when a storm hit Queensland in 2001. Steve and his best mate Wes had to get up in the middle of the night to clear debris. They were working as fast as they could when suddenly a 3.5-m (11.5-ft) crocodile leapt out of the water and sank its powerful jaws into Wes's leg.

'We took our eyes off Graham for a bit too long, and he came up behind me in waist-deep water and just drilled me into the fence,' said Wes in an interview for the *Sydney Morning Herald*. 'Luckily, he'd grabbed all meat, and when I twisted with all my might [the flesh] ripped clean out... He was about to grab me on the head when Steve leapt on his tail and hung on. I jumped out of the water onto the fence and I could see Steve jamming a stick into Graham's mouth. I yelled, "I'm clear!", and Steve's gone, "You beauty!", and he jumped out, too.'

It could have been a lot worse but Wes needed 150 stitches and was left with large holes in his leg. Nevertheless, he didn't bear a grudge. 'He had every right to attack. He was protecting his mate from invaders,' he said.

Steve's friends and family often testified how loyal and protective of them he was. Philippe Cousteau, who was with Steve on his last fateful trip told the US talkshow host Larry King that he was amazed how much the people around him loved Steve. 'They were... his family,' he said, 'and I have never seen a closer group of people that were more dedicated to each other, and he was so humble and just part of the team.'

Just like any family, they could also be merciless in their practical jokes and ribbing. 'Steve loved a practical joke,' John Stainton said

Steve Irwin on TV

Crocodile Hunter: The original Steve Irwin series following his exploits as he save crocodiles and other dangerous (and endangered) animals. (1996)

The Ten Deadliest Snakes in the World: Steve goes around the world searching out the world's most dangerous snakes in their natural habitat. (1998)

Croc Files: A series following Steve's animals both in the wild and at the animal sanctuary at Australia Zoo. (1999)

The Crocodile Hunter Diaries: A behind-the-scenes look at Steve's every-day life at Australia Zoo. (2002)

Island of Snakes: Steve goes to Sri Lanka to confront some of the most venomous snakes in the world and the man-eating Mugger crocodile. (2004)

Ice Breaker: Steve travels to Antarctica to meet penguins, leopard seals and humpback whales. (2004)

Search for a Super Croc: He hires a helicopter to capture nine monster crocs in order to study their movements in the wild. (2004)

Crocs in the City: Steve heads to Mexico to help deal with problem crocs in the resort towns of Tampico and Cancun. (2004)

Tigers of Shark Bay: He goes to Western Australia's Shark Bay to feed deadly bull sharks and then learns how to trap a monster Tiger shark in a plastic bag. (2004)

Confessions of the Crocodile Hunter: Interviews and behind-the-scenes footage of the Crocodile Hunter. (2004)

New Breed Vets: Steve explores the world of animal heart-transplants, fish contact lenses and other modern miracles of veterinary medicine. (2005)

in a newspaper tribute, recalling a rare occasion when he managed to get one over on the crocodile hunter by telling him that a wealthy sheikh was coming to visit the zoo.

'He was bowing and calling him "your majesty" – he was completely like a fish out of water,' John remembered. 'Then I had the sheikh say he wanted to see the camels. Now, the two camels at Australia Zoo were Steve's pride and joy. He loved them, really, really loved them. So I had the sheikh say through the translator that he wanted those camels. Steve was devastated, completely taken aback and he was trying to say that no, unfortunately, the sheikh couldn't have them and the translator was saying, "No, the sheikh wants those camels – he must have them." When we let him in on the joke, Steve never forgave me and never stopped trying to get me back.'

Chapter 4

Family Man

Steve was born on his mum's birthday and he always had a close relationship with both his parents. Their dream for an animal sanctuary became his dream and they could hardly believe what he'd achieved.

'I love my parents just so much, mate,' he once told the chat show host Andrew Denton. 'When I was the tiniest little kid... I'd look up at my dad and he was larger than life, he was just like this action hero. He was everything I wanted to be. And all I've done in my life is follow in his footsteps, mimic him and try to be him.'

His relationship with his family was always inseparable from his relationship with animals. His parents were first drawn together by their love of wildlife and it

ABOVE: Steve and Terri in Sydney, 2002.

LEFT: Steve's father Bob Irwin, who is also a naturalist and conservationist.

Steve with the second addition to the family, Bob.

was exactly the same when Steve met Terri. It would be hard to imagine either of them having a relationship with somebody who didn't feel the same way. Terri always believed that her habit of rescuing injured raccoons scared off boys back in Oregon, and Steve said of their meeting: 'I was no stud. I was obsessed by wildlife and hopeless with women, but Terri was as passionate about animals as me and the spark was unbelievable.'

When they had their first child, on July 24th 1998, they named her Bindi Sue after Steve's favourite crocodile Bindi and his much loved dog Sui. Sui the dog was born on Christmas Day 1988. Steve brought her home six weeks later and they were almost inseparable until she died ten years later.

Like Steve, Sui had been through the mill a bit. She was once impaled through the eye and out of the ear on a boar's tusk, she 'died' on the operating table in 1990 and only recovered thanks to a blood transfusion from a dog belonging to Steve's sister Mandy, she snapped a cruciate ligament in a car crash, she was impaled on a stake that she ran into after chasing a rat and she lost a lung after swallowing poison. The veterinary miracles that were performed on her probably inspired Steve's later *New Breed Vets* programme.

Despite all this she always seemed to have enormous love for the Irwin family and particularly for her namesake.

'It was so funny no one was allowed to muck with Bindi while Sui was guarding her,' Steve said on his website. 'We lost count how many times Bindi fell asleep on top of a very, very patient Sui.'

After surviving all that, Sui eventually died of cancer at home with Steve and Steve's best mate, Wes. 'On Wednesday 23rd of June Sui passed away in mine and Wes's arms,' Steve reported on the site. 'It hurt so,

Bindi meets *Sesame Street's* Bert and Ernie, as they pay a visit to Australia Zoo.

so much. We cried unbearably for hours as we dug a hole in her backyard and laid her to rest. God bless her soul. Her spirit will live forever.'

If that is how he felt about his dog it's not hard to imagine how he felt about his children. He once described Bindi Sue as 'the reason he was put on the Earth', and Terri often reminded people that 'the only thing that could ever keep him away from the animals he loves are the people he loves even more'.

A few years after Bindi was born Steve and Terri decided to try for another child and this time they hoped they'd have a boy. Typically, though, they went a bit beyond hoping. In crocodiles the temperature of the nest determines whether a croc is born male or female and they seemed to think that a similar thing might be true of humans!

Terri went to see a specialist in Melbourne who gave them some suggestions for the best way to increase their likelihood of having a boy. This meant eating a special diet, high in salt and with no dairy

Baby Bob.

products. Steve also had to take special measures, which apparently included giving up wearing underpants! 'You've got to get airflow round your testicles, see?' he told an embarrassed Andrew Denton. 'When you look at athletes, you know, 'cause their testicles are always hot, that they throw girl babies. Apparently the warm sperm are girl sperm and the cool ones are boy sperm.'

This was quite a sacrifice for somebody who spent a lot of their time in mosquito-infested swamps. 'In my line of work, seriously – good-fitting underpants are very, very important,' he laughed.

Whether all this made any difference or not they did have a boy. Robert Clarence Irwin, named after his two grandfathers, was born on 1st December 2003. The whole family were delighted although one member did have some reservations. Bindi Sue had grown up being told what a 'naughty boy' her dad had been when he was young. Steve's sisters, Mandy and Joy, were always telling her what they'd been through and she wasn't sure she wanted to go through the same thing!

Like their parents, though, both Bindi Sue and Bob were brought up around animals and they are just as fearless. 'We've got a daughter who's growing up like Mowgli out of the *Jungle Book*,' Steve once said.

The first time Bindi appeared on screen was with rattlesnakes in Texas when she was just two weeks old and it could have been even earlier than that. John Stainton and his crew were there at the birth! 'I kept 'em up the head of the bed,' said Steve, 'while I did the hard bit, you know popping the head out and everything.'

As a result she's become equally at home with TV crews and dangerous animals. In 2006 she began filming her first series, a 26-episode TV show for Animal Planet network in which she sings, dances, interviews celebrities and gets up close with wildlife just like her dad.

Steve and Terri looking forward to the arrival of their second child.

Steve with a baby tiger and Bindi – 'the reason he was put on earth'.

'The only thing that could ever keep him away from the animals he loves are the people he loves even more,' as Terri often said.

Steve with his family.

'When people clap and cheer me, it makes me happy because I feel I've done something well,' she told *Women's Weekly* magazine. 'When I grow up, I want to be doing exactly what I do now: sing, act and work with animals.'

Understandably, the Irwins were slightly concerned that their unusual life might make Bindi big-headed.

'We've connected a big green cord from the ground to Bindi's butt to keep her earthed!' Steve said in the same interview. 'She has celebrity parents, lives half the year in America and the other half in a zoo with 1,000 animals. She travels to amazing places, is part of a multi-million-dollar conservation foundation. It'd be easy for her to develop an "I-don't-need-to-work, I'll-do-whatever-the-hell-I-want" mindset, thinking that life's only about fun. That just ain't true. Bindi has to earn her own money. She has to earn respect.'

Despite this, there are some things in the lives of the children that, inevitably, aren't quite normal. In the Australia Zoo, they sell Steve and Terri action dolls and they were slightly disconcerted when Bindi started playing with them. 'She'll have them out playing and talking to them, saying "okay Mummy and Daddy, now you have to go to bed and go to sleep",' Terri said, 'and then she pretends to be us saying "No, no, we don't want to go to bed"… that's a bit surreal!'

The Irwins took great pride in watching Bindi developing into a 'Wildlife Warrior', but Steve acknowledged that she wasn't quite the same as him.

'I reckon she's a bit smarter than I was,' he told Andrew Denton. 'I don't know what it's like having a boy, but they don't seem incredibly intelligent till they reach 30. Really, I wasn't all that intelligent till I reached 30!'

Like father, like daughter, though. Bindi was bitten by a snake for the first time when she was just five years old. And this was a snake that Steve had only just saved from being run over as it slithered across the road.

'She starts wining "I want the snake!",' he remembered to Andrew. '"All right, sweetheart, but watch out, he's a bit bitey," She grabs it and she starts singing, "Rock-a-bye, baby", like this. It goes whack! Bites her right on the lip… I said, "told you he would bite you." She's like, "It's OK, Dad. Rock-a-bye…" Whack! Right on the nose. She goes, "Let it go, Dad." Gave it back to me. There's blood all pouring down there. I was very proud of her.'

In the same interview he admitted to being terrified by the realisation that his father wouldn't be around for ever. Steve's parents believed that he would be a

Bindi at two years old, happily playing with Burmese pythons.

Steve and Bindi with three-year-old Russ the alligator.

star long before he got anywhere near a camera and the desire to please them was a big part of his later success.

'First off, mate, bein' a bloke from the bush, I never knew I'd ever get this far,' he once said, 'but certainly my mum and dad knew that I was going to go to the top of the heap. To be truthful, I'm a little stunned that it's been this fast.'

Even as an adult he still craved the approval of his parents and they were delighted with what he'd made of their tiny Reptile Park. 'It almost makes me cry when Steve's father Bob visits the zoo,' the director Wes Mannion told the *Sydney Morning Herald*, 'because he's

just so proud of what Steve has done. And I think his approval means more to Steve than practically anything.'

The darkest moment of Steve's life came when his mother died in a car accident in 2002. 'I have never felt pain like that in my entire life,' he said. 'And what it did for me was it actually hammered home the whole family value thing… I was down for the count. I was down for two years. I was down. Way down.'

Throughout this it was his relationship with Terri that kept him going. When they could they did everything together, appearing side by side on screen and running the zoo. Without her drive it's equally

Steve with his mother Lyn, relocating a crocodile at the zoo.

Bindi's life is very different to that of most kids her age. Here she arrives at the premiere of her parents' film, *The Crocodile Hunter*.

The family celebrate Bob's second birthday.

Steve's last crocodile hunt, with his father, Bob, and Bindi.

Baby Bob and Bindi.

Steve with one of his elephants at Australia Zoo.

unlikely that he would ever have become such a big star. 'I am the business side,' she once admitted. 'I am the marketing and promotion side. I'm the straight man who plays off of the wild man. I'm Jane, he's Tarzan. It's always been like that. But I think that this is the spice of life. That is what's so exciting, and that's why people tune in.'

She was often asked how she could stand watching her husband do such a dangerous job. What they failed to realise was that, very often, she was with him.

'Say my husband had a dangerous job and I wasn't with him,' she said. 'I don't know how you go, "Oh honey, how was it with the police department today? You got all your fingers and toes today?" It would scare me. I'd have to become a police officer and work with him; I couldn't do it.'

For Terri, though, the demands of the family are more immediate than they were for Steve. She has talked about how she was once helping him fit satellite tracking devices on a crocodile when baby Bob started crying for a feed. This would have been fine except at the time she was lying on top of the croc to keep it still! 'Someone had to take my place on the croc,' she remembered. 'I was covered in mangrove mud and here's this beautiful clean baby being carried in a backpack by one of our assistants – I had to work out how to feed him without getting mud all over him!'

Ten years after they were married the Irwins might have felt that they deserved the honeymoon that they missed out on in 1992. But, typically, they spent their 10th wedding anniversary helping Indonesian elephants. Just like Steve's parents their relationship was founded on animal conservation and they didn't let anything else get in the way.

Terri in the croc enclosure at the family zoo.

Steve and Terri shared every part of their life together, as co-directors of Australia Zoo, as TV and film stars and as parents.

Terri Irwin

Terri acquired her business skills and her love of animals from her father. Like Steve she idolised her dad. He was an ex-policeman and World War II pilot, the 'biggest, strongest, bravest man' she knew.

He ran a successful construction business in Oregon, USA, and because he often brought home injured animals she became interested in helping them. There wasn't much else to do where they lived. She was much younger than her two sisters and often ended up amusing herself.

Unlike most children, though, her interests often revolved around making money by starting her own little businesses. Through selling lemonade and cleaning cars she eventually saved enough money to buy a horse.

'I've always been a capitalist, an unabashed capitalist,' she once said, 'and I always tell Steve that, if you want to save the world, then you have to charge more then $6 admission.'

In 1986, when she was 22, she started an animal sanctuary called 'Cougar Country' to help animals like bears, bob-cats and cougar prepare for the wild. She also went on holiday to Australia for the first time, falling in love with the country before reluctantly returning home. Then, three years later, wanting to get more involved with the animals, she trained as a veterinary technician.

'I remember I could budget $100 a month in groceries, I was thin back then,' she once said, 'and if I had a choice I would sit down at the end of the day with $5 and I could either feed myself or my cougar – I would feed my cougar.'

In 1991 she was still heavily involved with the family firm while looking after 300 animals a year, not including her own 15 cats, several birds and a dog. In October of that year, though, her friend Lori invited her on another trip to Australia. While there she spent much of her time investigating the country's approach to the rehabilitation of wildlife. She'd never heard of the Irwins' zoo. It was just complete coincidence that they happened to be driving past on a trip to the nearby Glasshouse Mountains as Steve was about to start his daily crocodile demonstration.

She found his stories of wrestling crocs into his boat captivating, but, as she recounts in *The Crocodile Hunter*, she couldn't think of a way to get his attention. Then she noticed that Lori had started talking to him. She walked over to join her friend and four months later she and Steve were engaged – four months after that they were married.

Chapter 5

Australian Icon to Global Phenomenon

By 2000 Steve Irwin was a huge star. John Stainton often commented that people in Australia didn't realise how famous he was overseas. When he flew into the US he'd have people waiting for him at the airport, his limousine would be followed and what he called 'radical fans' would be camped out outside his hotel. Occasionally, he had to call the police just so he could get out of his hotel room safely.

OPPOSITE: A-list celebrity and red-carpet regular, Steve at the premiere of *Master and Commander* in Los Angeles.
LEFT: It was Bruce Willis who first suggested to Steve that he should make a film.

Steve and Terri hit the big screen: *The Crocodile Hunter: Collision Course.*

He never complained, though. He took every chance he was offered to raise his profile and spread his message about conservation further. Incredibly, it was the Hollywood star Bruce Willis who pushed him to take the next step.

'Listen, if you guys have got a message,' he told Steve, 'take it to the big screen; it's the most powerful thing.'

So that year, he made a cameo appearance in Eddie Murphy's *Dr Doolittle 2.* Then in 2002 he made his own Hollywood film, *The Crocodile Hunter: Collision Course.* On paper it seemed like a ridiculous idea. Steve wasn't an actor. He was famous just for being himself. This might have been OK if it was a feature-length version of his TV shows, but it wasn't. It was a proper movie with a fantastical plot. A crocodile has stolen a top-secret US satellite beacon and CIA agents are sent to retrieve it. Unfortunately, Steve thinks that they're poachers and he does everything he can to stop them messing with his beloved croc.

Understandably, most critics weren't over-enamoured with the plot, but they were impressed by Steve. The director John Stainton's master-plan was, as ever, just to let Steve be himself, wrestling crocodiles, handling bird-eating spiders and venomous snakes as usual.

'Forget the plot,' said respected critic Roger Ebert. 'The movie is really about Steve and Terri

Steve and Terri's charm and energy lay at the heart of the film's appeal.

taking us on a guided tour of the crocs, snakes, deadly insects and other stars of the outback fauna.'

'The movie is entertaining exactly on the level I have described it,' he continued. 'You see a couple of likable people journeying though the outback, encountering dangerous critters and getting too close for comfort, while lecturing us on their habits and dangers and almost being killed by them. The stunts are not faked, and so there is a certain fascination.'

The Washington Post took exactly the same view. 'When I say this movie's a charm, I'm really talking about Irwin,' their critic commented.

John Stainton was determined that the film should allow Steve to be as natural as possible and he

went to extreme measures to prevent him being tied down by the business of 'acting'.

'I wasn't allowed on set, I wasn't allowed to read the script and I wasn't allowed to see the rushes,' Steve said. 'John wanted me to float through the movie, be totally myself and be a little naïve. So, even though my feelings were a little hurt by that, I knew it was all for the good of the final product.'

The fact that they didn't use stunt men, plastic crocs or CGI also gave it a realism that most Hollywood films don't have. 'I got busted up a lot doing the film,' he admitted. 'There was a lot of blood, my face got caved in by a female croc underwater, I had a cartilage operation in the middle

No rubber crocodiles were used during filming.

Steve and Terri were encouraged by director John Stainton just to be themselves.

Not all the actors on the film were as happy as Steve to get up close to crocs.

of it all – so that all got edited down so that kids could watch it.'

Understandably some of the other actors were less keen on getting up close with the crocodiles. Fans have pointed out that when the fat lady ends up in the water with the crocodile you can see that it isn't her: it's Steve in an unconvincing fat suit and wig.

The film eventually took a respectable US$33 million in its opening weekend and it should have been the pinnacle of his career. It was during the filming, though, that his mother was killed in that tragic accident. Steve immediately went into a deep depression, but he tried to see the movie as a tribute to her. 'She really wanted us to make a movie the whole family could get excited about,' he said.

'My mum used to complain, years ago, about people sitting around the idiot box watching different shows,' he said in an interview with the journalist Paul Fischer. 'Now, for the first time in a long time, the whole family, from little toddlers to the kids to teenagers and mums and dads and, by crikey, even great grandpa and grandma, can sit down and watch

As Steve did all the stunts himself, the film had a realism that most Hollywood films can't even aspire to.

this flick, and be totally excited and have more fun than you can have in two hours anywhere.'

By then the zoo and his TV programmes had given Steve everything he ever wanted and he was able to plough all of the profits from *Collision Course* back into his conservation charities. He'd been planning to make a film since 1995, even before the TV series first appeared in America, but his experiences of Hollywood weren't all positive.

'Where I live,' he commented after the filming process, 'if someone gives you a hug it's from the heart. I've had these blokes in Hollywood hug me trying to make out I'm their friend and as soon as I turn their back they take out a big bunch of knives and stab me in the back. I feel sorry for these people because they are so shallow.'

The point of the film, then, was purely to raise money and raise the profile of conservation issues. After Steve's death the radio presenter Jono Coleman said, 'I found him to be completely focused and obsessed when it came to his environmental causes and the promotion of Australia and its rare and bizarre animals and creatures.'

Two Australian icons. Dame Edna pays a visit to Australia Zoo.

Not that there weren't other perks of being famous. He proudly told interviewers that the film company MGM had bought him 22 new safari suits. 'I've still got dozens of them left in the packs,' he laughed to Andrew Denton. 'Talk about rip off the big people, eh? It's all about what falls off the back of the truck!'

By now he was such a big star he was even invited to Bill Clinton's farewell dinner at the end of his presidency. He turned the invitation down, but a few years later he had the opportunity to meet another US President when the Australian Prime Minister John Howard invited him to a barbecue in honour of George W. Bush.

This high profile inevitably meant he was a target for satirists and comedians everywhere. The adult cartoon *South Park* famously sent him up in the 'Prehistoric Iceman' episode by portraying him diving in with a crocodile and promising to 'shove my thumb right up its butt hole'.

Characteristically, Steve found it hilarious. 'We nearly died laughing,' he told *Scientific American*. 'Honestly, I loved that,' he said. 'You know, I'm Australian, and we have got the worst sense of humour. We are cruel to each other. *South Park* was excellent, really. Imagine how you can back our message, whether the animators agree or not, taking our message to *South Park* and touching millions of people around the world with animation.'

As well as this Steve also appeared, or was sent up on, *The Basil Brush Show, The Muppet Show, The Simpsons*, and many others.

This might be why the Irwins decided that their next step would be to make their own animated series. At least that way Steve could just leave the creative work to somebody else and get on with looking after the zoo. While some people might have thought that Steve was in love with the big screen he always saw it as just a means to an end.

'We didn't really act in this movie and we're not Hollywood actors,' he said. 'Blokes like Bruce Willis, Matt Damon and Will Smith are the real Hollywood stars and, by crikey, it's a tough job they do and they can have it.'

Although he respected what they did Steve had never been particularly impressed with that world. Even when he was kid his biggest hero was the French ecologist and pioneering natural-history documentary maker Jacques Cousteau.

'What he did for conservation in the 60s through the 70s was just phenomenal,' Steve said. 'And I want to be just like him, you know?'

This meant going beyond appearances on the screen. At the Australia Zoo the Irwins had a huge

Jacque Cousteau was a childhood hero of Steve's.

range of merchandise, from the action dolls mentioned earlier to a range of children's clothing named in honour of Bindi. All of the profits went directly into conservation and the Irwins' conservation war-chest was growing all the time.

'You know, easily the greatest threat to the wildlife globally is the destruction of habitat,' Steve said. 'So I've gone, "Right, well, how do I fix that?"

On a tour of the States to promote *The Crocodile Hunter*, Steve stops off at San Francisco Zoo to pose with an alligator.

Steve and Terri with their 'Crikey' licence plate.

Well, making a quid here. People are keen to give me money over there. I'll buy it. I'll buy habitat.'

Whenever they could, the Irwins bought great chunks of land all over the world to turn into conservation parks. They were also heavily involved in more immediate conservation issues. After the battle for independence in East Timor they flew out to the country and were shocked to discover that two crocodiles, the sacred symbol of East Timor, were being kept in dreadfully inhumane conditions. There was talk of relocating the crocs to Australia, but

Steve had always been taught by his father to respect whatever people regarded as sacred and so he insisted that they remain in the country. Instead, the Australia Zoo funded two new enclosures for them. After the conflict those enclosures were the first new buildings to be built in East Timor by anybody.

Steve was ecstatic, but the more sensible Terri pointed out that some of the East Timorese people might be a little put out that they were spending money on crocs when some people still didn't have homes! In response, they found thousands of dollars

Steve's passion for the natural world was not just a show for the cameras. He was a naturalist, not a circus act.

to pay for a new medical centre. At the same time they also tried to cheer up the next generation and encourage them to love animals by giving the children rubber snakes and toy crocodiles.

'Everyone's worried about feeding the children and clothing the children and medicating the children, but they're forgetting that they're children,' said Steve to *Scientific American*. 'We gave them little animals to be proud of and excited about. I think that it is a long process, but that it is a start. And, like with our shows, we're not cramming it down their heads. It's becoming cool, and it's a whole new thought process.'

In dealing with developing countries, Steve had come to realise that it wasn't enough just to tell people to love animals. It was unreasonable to ask poor or even starving people to worry about snakes and crocodiles. Instead, the Australia Zoo got involved with projects that were about helping people and animals at the same time. One example was 'gorilla-friendly bananas' where banana farmers would receive a better price for their product if they didn't shoot the gorillas that came to eat part of their crop.

Despite all the problems in the world Steve was optimistic that his message was getting across.

'What I'm currently seeing with my own eyes is fantastic,' he said. 'I think global awareness in terms of conservation is really starting to come into the fore of people's brains, rather than the arse. That's exciting, and I'm seeing quite a massive global push towards wildlife conservation.'

After conservation Steve's other main passion was for his country, Australia. He was always more than willing to help promote tourism and, rather than ask for a fee, he merely asked for a donation to his wildlife charity. In typical style, at a 'Visit Australia' marketing push at the University of California in Los Angeles, he told an audience of Americans, 'Mate, it's easy. You get on to Qantas, watch a few movies, sip a few Australian wines, have a slash, a sleep and you're there.'

For a long time there was a debate within the Australian tourism industry about whether they wanted to be promoting Australia with seemingly old-fashioned stereotypes about mateship, crocs, barbecues and 'roos. By 2000, though, Steve was probably the most recognisable symbol of the country for the rest of the world and, really, they had no choice.

Robert Hunt, a senior executive at Invest Australia, said, 'There are people – not me – who get quite upset with campaigns that identify Australia with kangaroos, beaches and beer. I used to be one of those people, but I'm not as upset by that any more. Anything that raises awareness of Australia is probably good.'

But Steve's concern for tourism may also have been, essentially, a way to get people interested in looking after wildlife. 'People are not going to travel thousands of miles to just get a café latte in Australia,' he pointed out in one interview. 'They

Demonstrating with a bird of prey at Mogo Zoo.

are going to come here to see our unique wildlife like our kangaroos, wombats, platypuses and our beaches and rainforests. This is the only place on earth they can see these things in their natural environment. And if they do get a good café latte on their way out then that's a bonus!'

A hugely popular spokesperson, Steve launches Perth Mint's 'Discover Australia' collector coin programe, in January 2006.

Steve's everyday life was literally the stuff of Hollywood films.

Thinking Globally

Steve's *Crocodile Hunter* series had an estimated audience of 500 million worldwide.

His film *The Crocodile Hunter: Collision Course* grossed US$33 million worldwide.

Steve's daughter Bindi Sue Irwin had been on over 300 flights by her 5th birthday.

Steve and Terri have bought land in Fiji, Vanuatu, the USA and Australia to make it safe for wildlife.

By 2006 they had bought approximately 36,420 hectares (90,000 acres) of land.

In 2002 alone *Business Review Weekly* magazine estimated that Steve made A$16.3 million.

In 2004, Steve Irwin invested A$40 million in Australia Zoo.

Australia Zoo employs more than 400 people and is one of Queensland's most popular tourist destinations.

Justin Timberlake and the 2000 US Olympics team are among many fans who have been to Australia Zoo.

The *Crocodile Hunter* TV series has been shown in 140 different countries.

A star draw at Nickelodeon's Annual Kids' Choice Awards in Santa Monica, California, 2002, Steve handles a snake on stage.

Chapter 6

Controversy

When Steve became one of Australia's biggest stars there was inevitably an element of tall poppy syndrome. Despite his down-to-earth character there were those who felt embarrassed about the image of their country that he projected world-wide. When Australia was trying to present itself as a dynamic, modern nation here was this guileless larrikin dragging the country back to the days of *Crocodile Dundee*. He thought that many of his fellow countrymen were simply embarrassed about him. 'I'm very embarrassing to look at,' he told Andrew Denton. 'You know why? Here's why I'm embarrassing. Because there's a little bit of me in everybody. There really is, you know? I'm like the boy that never grew up.'

A star, yes, but not everyone was comfortable the larrikin image the 'Crocodile Hunter' presented to the world.

Steve takes Bob into the crocodile enclosure, January 2004.

That was certainly the attitude of the Federal Industry Minister Ian MacFarlane. In 2002 he accused Steve of 'trying to wind back the clock' on Australia's tourism industry. 'We've seen Australia evolve from a destination with the sophistication of a crocodile wrestler,' he said. 'Steve Irwin the Crocodile Hunter may be trying to wind the clock back, but I hope we've moved beyond that for the sake of our tourism.'

The Queensland Premier Peter Beattie initially agreed, complaining that he wanted Australia to be known for more than just a man who wrestled crocs.

To begin with, though, Steve's astonishing success gave detractors few opportunities to cut him down. He was accused of teasing or provoking the animals that he interacted with, but nobody could argue with his record of conservation.

Steve insisted that his son was in no danger.

Then in 2004 two major incidents tested his popularity for the first time. In January he faced a storm of controversy after being filmed holding his baby son, Bob, in one hand while feeding a chicken carcass to a 4-m (13-ft) croc with the other. It was just the kind of schooling he'd had from his own father. 'It's about time Bob got out there,' he said, but a spokesman for the Childhood Foundation was outraged. 'It's neglect,' said the foundation's Joe Tucci. 'I don't think we should use children as props, and definitely not in situations that are going to put them in such danger.'

On reflection, Steve realised how bad it must have looked to people watching. 'If I could have my time again I would probably do things differently,' he said. But he was always adamant that Bob had been

his Antarctica documentary *Icebreaker* there were complaints that he was getting a little too close to the wildlife. The promotional material for the show promised: 'he slides down hillsides with penguins, almost rubs noses with the notoriously dangerous Leopard seals and spends the most inspiring time with two friendly Humpback whales'.

There are international laws about how close you can get to animals in the Antarctic. The rules state that visitors to Antarctica must stay at least 5 m (16 ft) from seals and penguins. Swimming with whales is banned. The maximum penalty is either fines of up to $1 million or even two years in jail.

Once again, he was investigated by his own government, but this time he strongly protested his innocence. Environmental officials decided not to press charges, but for some that wasn't the end of the matter. Greenpeace weren't convinced and the campaigner Quentin Hanich demanded that Animal Planet release the whole, unedited footage of Steve's trip.

'If Steve Irwin and the government want to make the case that there's nothing to answer, then the easiest way of doing that is releasing the tape,' he said. 'There are many scientists and environmental organisations around Australia that specialise in whale watching and there are great sustainable whale-watching organisations in Australia that have a lot of expertise in the matter. Show the tape and they'll comment.'

Part of the problem was that Steve had a close relationship with the Australian Prime Minister John Howard and there were allegations that he'd been treated leniently because of his celebrity. At the end of 2003 John Howard had visited Australia Zoo and Steve shocked everyone by declaring: 'In front of us right now is the greatest leader Australia has ever had and the greatest leader in the world.'

'I've travelled the world,' he continued, 'I've been to areas of conflict, I've been to the Sari Club (in Bali) and there I see the Prime Minister backing it up as a fair dinkum Australian like no other Prime Minister has ever done for this country.'

'It's great to be in the company of one of Australia's great conservation icons,' Howard replied. 'People are instinctively drawn to people that are regarded as an authentic Australian – a love of bushland, a love of nature, a commitment to openness and a welcoming face.'

Perhaps naively Steve hadn't realised that this endorsement would immediately make him public enemy number one for those people who didn't like John Howard or his party. 'I love John Howard,' he said defiantly, 'and that's the way I am.'

Nevertheless, he didn't want to be associated in the public eye with any one political party. 'I'm sitting on the fence, mate,' he said. 'I'm a conservationist. I can't afford to be one way or the other. I just have to run straight up the middle, mate. I have to get on with whoever's in power.'

When it was put to Howard that he might have been lenient towards Steve Irwin because he was a celebrity the Prime Minister answered, 'That is an absurd thing to say. The matter was examined properly and that was the conclusion.'

Steve tried to brush off the investigation as 'just a big storm in a teacup', but he felt that he had been treated unfairly over the matter. 'How dare I kiss a Leopard seal on the lips while others are out there clubbing Harp seals to death?' he said sarcastically. But to someone who refused to holiday in Canada because 'that's where they whack baby seals' the allegation that he was harming them was very hurtful.

Steve welcomes Prime Minister John Howard to Australia Zoo.

More seriously, Steve alleged that he had received death threats after his campaigns against the exploitation of wildlife and he wondered aloud whether these new allegations came from the same source. In the end, though, he was too thick-skinned to pay much attention to what people said about him.

'I'm very proud of what I do and I'll die doin' it,' he told Andrew Denton with eerie prescience. 'And basically, mate, I don't give a rip what anybody thinks; I do not care. I've got a message that's goin' out to 5 million people right now, this moment on the television, and, crikey, who knows how many people will watch the movie. I've got more important things to think about than what others think of me.'

Even before he died, however, there were still those who thought that he was a hero – particularly the family of a diving instructor called Scott Jones who was once saved by Steve Irwin.

Steve performs in front of John Howard, whom he described as the 'greatest leader in the world'.

Philosophical under fire. Steve photographed at Australia Zoo amid reports that he could be under Federal Government investigation for a possible criminal breach of wildlife laws while filming in Antarctica.

The negative publicity didn't stick – Steve speaking at the POA Awards, in 2005.

The diver had been exploring with a small group of people off the coast of Mexico when a daring 77-year-old named Katie Vrooman got into trouble.

'It was on our first dive of the trip, and the dive-master of the operation took us on where we shouldn't have been for the first dive,' Scott told the American talkshow host Larry King, 'and there was rough current come up and people were getting separated.'

Katie was caught by the strong currents and bashed against the rocks as Scott desperately tried to save her.

'By the time I got to her,' Scott continued, 'another wave took her and got her again.' He tried to hold on to her unconscious body for as long as he could, almost two hours, but in the end she was swept away and he was stranded on a narrow ledge for the night.

Meanwhile, Steve was filming a documentary about sea lions off the coast of Mexico's Baja California Peninsula when he heard that the two scuba divers were reported missing. He immediately abandoned filming, used his satellite communications system to call for an air search and sent his team in kayaks to search the area.

One of the kayakers found Scott and Steve dived into the sea to pull him off the rock and back to his boat. He was battered and dehydrated and totally oblivious to who his rescuer was. 'Somebody behind me said, "So what do you think of the Crocodile Hunter?"' Scott recalled. 'So I was looking around for Crocodile Dundee. I thought when the makeup comes off Dundee's looks must change. But, when I finally got home my daughter turned the Animal Planet channel on and I started watching his show from then.'

Bindi congratulates her father on being named Queensland's Australian of the Year, November 2003. A nomination that was not withdrawn while welfare officers decided whether to take action against him in January 2004.

'He was very, very excited to be rescued but he was so sad and I feel so sorry for him and what a hero,' said Steve afterwards. 'He's the hero, mate, not me. I'm not the hero here. I'm just the bloke that, you know, helped him off the rock. He's the true hero hanging onto her in her passing from this life into the next wherever that may be.'

When Steve died Scott and his wife Debbie were devastated. They found it particularly sad that he was killed by a creature that they'd always loved.

'What's ironic to me is he would be killed by one of Scott's most favourite creatures of the underwater world,' Debbie said. 'He loves the stingrays. He feeds them, he plays with them. They are one of his favourites.'

After his rescue Scott had become a fan of the *Crocodile Hunter* shows, too, and he had great respect for Steve's work. 'He was a hell of an educator, from kids all the way up to old farts like me,' he said.

It's fair to say that not everybody thought the same way about Steve, but the Wildlife Warrior could give just as good as he got. The biggest battle in his life was against the growing trend towards what was called 'sustainable use' in conservation.

This doctrine holds that the best way to ensure the survival of wildlife was to allow a certain amount of exploitation. The theory was that, if people could make money out of whale blubber, say, they'd be more likely to support schemes to ensure that whale species weren't driven to extinction. It was an idea that disgusted Steve Irwin.

'I believe sustainable use is the greatest propaganda in wildlife conservation at the moment,' he told *Scientific American*. 'This propaganda has been established by some very credible, very powerful players, and it seems to me that people are using the camouflage of science to make money out of animals.'

'I understand that we've got to have trees to build houses, we've got to have roads, we've got to have farming, we've got to have grazing,' he continued, 'but I sincerely and vehemently oppose "sustainable use", where people think they can farm crocodiles and kill them, and turn them into boots, bags and belts. Killing any wild animal will never save it, regardless of what anyone says.'

Some people believed that this was too unsophisticated and the *Sydney Morning Herald* took particular issue with his claim that eating beef and lamb was more ethical than eating kangaroo and crocodile.

'Cows have been on our land for so long that Australia has evolved to handle those big animals,' Steve said, but the newspaper concluded that his message merely amounted to 'eating roos and crocs is bad for tourism, and therefore more cruel than eating other animals'.

The proprietors of the new crocodile farms didn't like his message much, either. Keith Cook, the proprietor of the Cairns Crocodile Farm, said, 'All it meant, in my eyes, was that he'd gone from a harmless buffoon to some sort of religious crusader, [whose] show has become a means of preaching to the gullible.'

Steve could take this kind of thing on the chin and give it back but he wasn't quite as immune to self-doubt as you might think. He also claimed that, initially, he had qualms about how he came across on screen.

'I started seeing things about myself in [*The Crocodile Hunter* TV series] that I didn't like, and I was starting to change,' he said.

Apparently, John Stainton warned him that

A crocodile farm. Steve was against the 'sustainable use' argument, proffered by crocodile farmers.

Steve felt there was no justification for farming crocodiles, and killing them for their skin.

As one of Australia's greatest ambassadors for tourism, Steve's image was emblazoned across a new locomotive for the Ghan service from Adelaide to Darwin in 2003. His status as an icon still remained during the following, more difficult, year.

that would be a disaster. 'He said if we were gonna prosper,' Steve continued, 'and do this for the rest of our lives, I had to stay the same as I was the first day we met.'

As a result he never watched the programmes until they went out on air. He trusted John to judge whether particular segments worked or not. 'That way,' Steve continued, 'I can travel through life just being me. 'Cause, deadset, the secret of our success is just havin' raw Stevo.'

Ultimately this tactic undoubtedly worked. Even after all the bad press Stevo was still in huge demand as a spokesman, whether by commercial sponsors, or the federal government. Despite the misgivings of some politicians there was no denying that his plain-speaking manner made him a uniquely trustworthy figurehead. It helped that he only lent his name to causes that he felt strongly about. Among other things he was the face of the Australian Quarantine and Inspection Service, which tried to prevent people bringing non-indigenous flora and fauna into the country.

'We're an island continent,' he said. 'We don't have foot and mouth disease, we don't have screw-worm, we don't have rabies. Let's keep it that way.'

Chapter 7

Tragedy

In January 2006 Steve appeared before a crowd in Los Angeles limping, with a brace on his left leg. He jokingly told the audience, there for a celebration of Australia Week, that he'd like to say he injured himself fighting white sharks but that actually he'd torn some ligaments while wrestling.

'I was training and I had my bodyguard on the ground, he had me in a leg lock and so I leant back to hit him and I twisted one way and as he put the leg lock on and twisted the other way – he pulled it straight out... it really hurt,' Steve said.

The joke was that by then everybody expected him to get injured in his line of work. He once estimated that he'd been bitten more than a 1,000 times. In interviews he often mentioned the possibility of his own death. He seemed to accept that one day he might be unlucky, but, for all that, there was an air of invincibility about him. Even those people who said 'he's going to get killed one day' must have admitted to being shocked in September 2006 when the tragic news of his death came through.

In 2006 he'd mostly put the controversy two years previous earlier behind him. He was starting to get more recognition for his conservation work and he was immensely proud that his daughter Bindi was about to star in her own series for the Junior Discovery Channel. He was also excited to be working with the grandson of his all-time hero Jacques Cousteau on a new series called *Ocean's Deadliest*. 'There'll be crocs, sharks and the world's most venomous creature, the Box jellyfish,' Steve told one interviewer not long before he set sail on *Croc 1*.

With Philippe Cousteau he headed out towards the Great Barrier Reef as planned but they weren't able to do much filming because of bad weather so they were mostly confined to the boat. 'Steve is not good with being confined to a boat for any length of time,' John Stainton said on Larry King's show immediately after the accident. 'And, when the sun came out yesterday morning, he said to me,

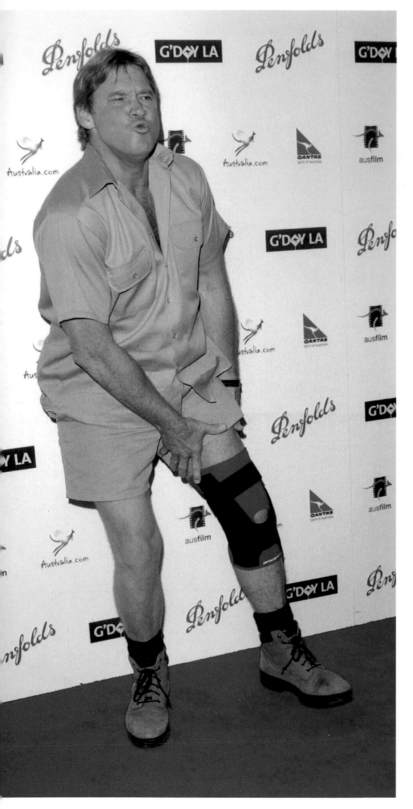

Steve joked about his leg injury, which happened while wrestling with his body guard, not a crocodile.

"Look, I might just go out and pick up a couple of segments for Bindi's new kids' show."'

With a cameraman Steve headed out on the *Rubber Ducky* dinghy in search of shots for Bindi's new show *Jungle Girl.* Not long afterwards, John received a call saying that there was an emergency and Medivac (the air ambulance) had been called.

'It was a blur as to what was happening,' John told Larry King. 'I didn't know who was hurt. I obviously did not think it would be Steve. I thought he was invincible, you know, that he was never going to be hurt badly, ever.'

Tragically, when Steve was pulled on board he was already unconscious. A helicopter flew in from nearby Cairns, but the only place it could land was on an island at least 20 minutes away. They sped towards it as fast as they could in the *Croc 1* boat, desperately trying to revive him, but John suspected that they were already too late. He was dead. According to Dr Ed O'Loughlin, who treated Steve, 'it became clear fairly soon that he had non-survivable injuries… He had a penetrating injury to the left front of his chest. He had lost his pulse and wasn't breathing.'

What had happened wasn't apparent until they watched the film afterwards. Steve and the cameraman had dived and somehow ended up swimming above a large, bull-nose stingray. After viewing the film, the marine documentary filmmaker Ben Cropp speculated that the stingray 'felt threatened because Steve was alongside and there was the cameraman ahead'.

For whatever reason the stingray lashed out with its deadly tail and the serrated barb at the end pierced his chest. It was an incredible piece of misfortune. Only three people have been killed by stingrays in Australian history. It was 'a one-in-a-million thing' Cropp told *Time* magazine.

The Great Barrier Reef – where Steve was filming when the tragic accident occurred.

Stingrays are known for their lack of aggression. In some parts of the world tourists have been allowed to hand-feed them. The fact that Steve, who'd swum with the world's most dangerous sharks and reptiles, was killed by a seemingly harmless ray shocked the world.

'He's been diving for, I don't know, ten, 15 years with sharks, with everything that would kill you in the water,' John said, 'but I never thought he'd take a hit from a stingray.'

'We had been about ten days or so into the shoot and things were going so well and I think that's, you know, the irony of the whole story was that stingrays weren't even part of the show,' Steve's co-presenter Philippe Cousteau said afterwards. Philippe found the death particularly shocking because his father also died suddenly in an accident, also leaving a widow, a daughter and a son.

While Steve's body was flown to a morgue in Cairns somebody had to call Terri. She was on a

The stingray's deadly tale has a serrated barb at the end, which pierced Steve's heart.

walking tour in Tasmania at the time and flew back by private plane immediately. More than anybody she knew the risks that Steve took, but more than anybody she had faith that he knew what he was doing. 'I think probably an average of once a week I'm afraid for my life or Steve's life,' she once said, 'but it is exciting because my husband literally saves my life from time to time and it's never a dull moment.'

While his family were still dealing with the terrible shock the question immediately arose of what to do about the tape of Steve's death. He'd often joked that if he was ever killed while filming he wanted the tape to carry on rolling. He wanted to go out saying 'crikey!' After the accident those jokes came back to haunt Steve's friends and family. John Stainton had to watch the tape to verify its contents for the police and he told Larry King, 'I would never want that tape shown. I mean it should be destroyed. At the moment, it's in police custody for evidence. There's a coroner's inquest taking place at the moment. And when that is finally released it will never see the light of day ever, ever.'

With Terri and the rest of Steve's family in deep mourning it fell on John Stainton to explain to Steve's shocked fans what had happened.

'I loved him dearly,' he told Larry King, 'and we had a partnership that was made in heaven. I mean he never interfered in my side of the business, which was making the television shows. I never interfered in his side of the business, which was jumping on crocodiles and I didn't want to do that anyway.'

'I have to do these interviews,' he continued. 'It's not my job to be in front of a camera but he did it for me for 15 years and never questioned it.'

The next issue was whether or not to accept the Australian government's offer of a state funeral. Steve's

Steve's great friend and manager, John Stainton, attends the memorial service held at Australia Zoo.

family and friends appreciated what an honour it was, but at the same time they didn't want his memorial to turn into a media circus. In the end Steve's dad said that he would have wanted to be remembered as an ordinary bloke and so they had a campfire service at Australia Zoo where the family and close friends sat around swapping stories.

Bob Irwin said, 'Because Steve loved the Bush so much and yarning around the campfire, the service was held just like he would have wanted, with everyone telling their favourite stories around a candlelit fire. It was what he would have wanted and it has brought some family closure to his life.'

However, many thousands of fans also wanted to pay their respects and it was decided to hold a public memorial at the 5,500-seater 'Crocoseum'

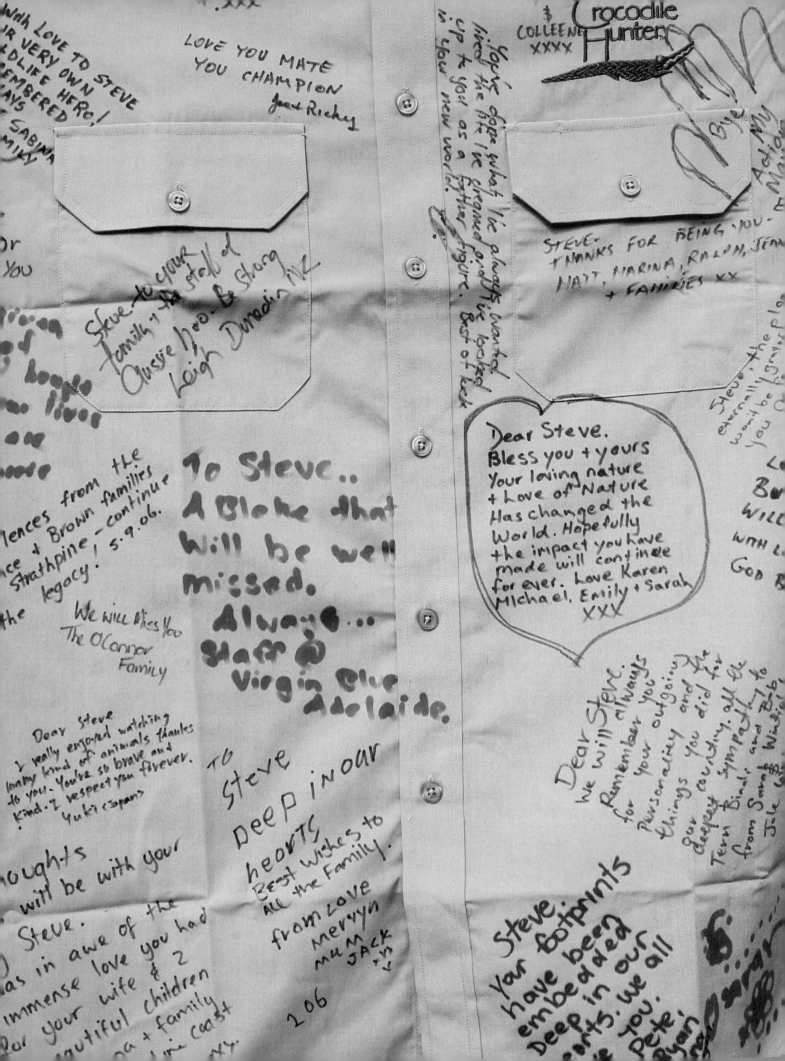

One of the many tributes left at Australia Zoo, as the tragic news broke.

at Australia Zoo, where Steve had enthralled and entertained so many people. Even then, so many people wanted to attend that the venue couldn't possibly hold all the people who wanted to be there. The tickets were taken in just 15 minutes, with some fans camping out in order to guarantee they were first in line, so big screens were erected at various locations around the country to broadcast it live.

Right up until the last minute it was unclear whether Terri and the rest of the family would feel able to speak. John Stainton admitted to Larry King that she was finding it incredibly hard. 'I think the fact that Steve was so young and has left two little kids, great kids behind, she'll have a hard time handling the children and getting them through the tragedy as well,' he said.

The private and public services reflected the two sides of Steve's character. Where the first was just his family and friends talking about what he meant to them, the second was a big, showbiz affair with

A tearful Terri, with Bindi and Bob, bids her final farewell.

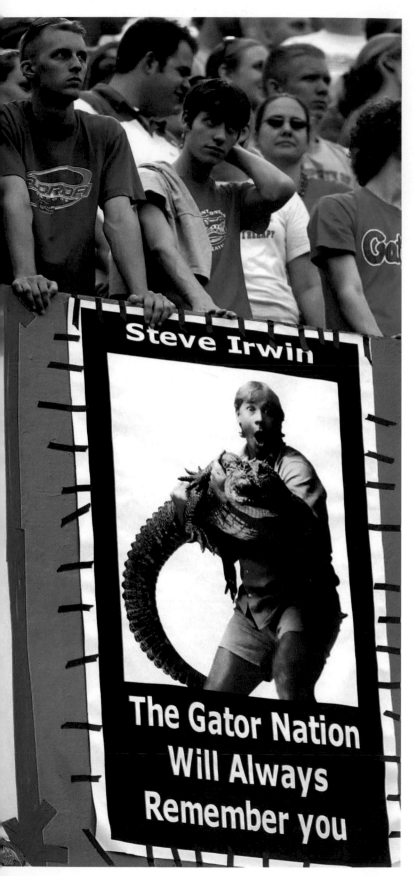

world-famous celebrities, politicians and an estimated audience of 300 million people worldwide. Inside the 'Crocoseum' all but one of the 5,500 seats was taken. They left Steve's old seat empty, marked with his cap.

The service began with a videotaped tribute from Steve's friend Russell Crowe in New York. 'I hope someone will speak of what Steve achieved as a conservationist but all I can do today is talk directly to my friend, my mate, Steve,' he said. 'Your passing has suspended reality for all of us. It was way too soon and completely unfair on all accounts. I know, as humble as you always were, that you would still be pleased to know that the world sends its love. We have all have been grieving. We have all lost a friend, we lost a champion and we are going to take some time to adjust to that.'

The Prime Minister John Howard then spoke for the Australian government. 'Steve Irwin touched the hearts of Australians and touched the hearts of millions around the world in a very special way,' he said. 'He did that because he had that quality of being genuine, of being authentic, of being unconditional and having a great zest for life.'

There were other recorded tributes sent in from all over the world from stars like Kevin Costner, Hugh Jackman, Justin Timberlake and Cameron Diaz. 'He was fearless,' said Costner. 'He let us see who he was. That is being brave in today's society.'

'America just flipped for him,' said Diaz. 'Every kid was in love with the idea of being him.'

'I'll never forget what I learned just by being around Steve,' Justin Timberlake added. 'Not even what he taught me, just what I learned by

John Howard paid tribute to Steve at the memorial service.

So many people turned up at Australia Zoo to pay their respects, the police had to impose traffic restrictions in the area.

'My daddy was a hero.' Bindy's brave, but heartbreaking, speech was unforgettable.

Utterly bereft: John Stainton and the beloved family Steve left behind.

being around him with animals. My thoughts and prayers are with all of you and he will definitely be missed.'

But in the end it was Bindi's speech that was most moving for the people at the Crocoseum and the millions watching on TV. 'My Daddy was my hero,' she said, 'he was always there for me when I needed him… I know that daddy made this zoo so everyone could come and learn to love all the animals,' she finished. 'Daddy made this place his whole life and now it's our turn to help daddy."'

The flags at Sydney Harbour Bridge flew at half-mast, Australia was virtually at a stand-still and John Williamson, one of Steve's favourite Australian singers sang his favourite song, 'True Blue', as Wes Mannion drove Steve's favourite truck out of the arena for the last time.

Wes Mannion.

Meanwhile, in America the Animal Planet network was taking the unprecedented step of broadcasting the memorial live at peak time without commercial breaks. The network owed Steve Irwin a huge debt and its parent company, the Discovery Channel, issued a statement from chairman John Hendricks. 'Steve was a larger-than-life force,' he said. 'He brought joy and learning about the natural world to millions and millions of people across the globe. We extend our thoughts and prayers to Terri, Bindi and Bob Irwin as well as to the incredible staff and many friends Steve leaves behind.'

They also announced that they would rename the garden space in front of Discovery's world headquarters in Silver Spring, Maryland, the 'Steve Irwin Memorial Sensory Garden'.

In a further, very Australian tribute, fans were urged to wear khaki for a day in memory of him. However, many people pointed out that by far the best memorial to him was Australia Zoo, his Wildlife Warriors Charity and his organisation's continuing charity work around the globe. TV naturalist Jack Hanna agreed, saying, 'the tribute is going to be what Steve left behind. And that's his magnificent zoological park and the memories that all of us will have of all his shows. And that's really what it boils down to in the end, whatever the tribute might be, it's what we're all going to remember him by, and he's left a great legacy.'

John Williamson sings from atop Steve's truck, surrounded by staff from Australia Zoo.

The world will never forget
the 'Crocodile Hunter'.

Could His Death Have Been Prevented?

After Steve's death the first reaction was shock, then people naturally wondered whether there was any way his death could have been prevented. Some people blamed the Discovery Channel for encouraging him to risk his life getting so close to wildlife, perhaps forgetting that he was wrestling crocodiles long before he had a camera with him. Some people, absurdly, blamed the stingray. There were reports of dead, mutilated stingrays washing up on Queensland's beaches. Many people, though, blamed Steve himself.

He always knew the risks he was taking and he accepted them. 'The only thing that I am a little concerned about is that Bindi won't have a daddy and that kind of worries me a little,' he once told Larry King.

Among naturalists his work had always been controversial. Many, like Britain's veteran David Bellamy were hugely supportive. 'The thing with Steve was he mixed damn good science with show business,' he said, 'and I don't know anyone else who did that.'

But his compatriot Ray Mears was less convinced. 'Dangerous animals, you leave them alone because they will defend themselves,' he said. 'Nature defends itself.'

The most scathing criticism came from the feminist intellectual Germaine Greer just a day after Steve's death. 'The animal world has finally taken its revenge,' she wrote, causing outrage in Australia.

A few days later a PETA activist (People for the Ethical Treatment of Animals), Dan Matthews, made similar comments. 'It comes as no shock at all that Steve Irwin should die provoking a dangerous animal,' he said. 'He made a career out of antagonising frightened wild animals, which is a very dangerous message to send to kids.'

While Steve Irwin's fans may have disagreed with these comments, there may also have been some guilt at the enjoyment we all gained from watching him dice with death. He once estimated that he'd been bitten over 1,000 times. Although his death may have been a terrible one-in-a-million accident, the odds on him being killed or seriously injured by something must have been considerably shorter than that.

One reason he took such risks was that he knew it made people watch his show and it enabled him to get his message across to as many people as possible. 'It's not like these scars are trophies, mate,' he told Larry King. 'It's like they're interesting and it helps me to prompt talk about conservation.'

Steve was not the naïve bushman that he pretended to be. He made his choices and he lived and died by them. One of the criticisms that he most relished was that he was an 'adrenaline junky'.

'I get called an adrenaline junkie every other minute,' he told Scientific American, 'and I'm just fine with that. You know what though, mate? I'm doing exactly what I've done from when I was a small boy. You can blame my dad for that, he started it. He created me. He nurtured my instincts and he caused me to be who I am, so I've followed in his footsteps. All I ever wanted was to be my dad, so yeah, I applaud that. Thrill-seeker, adrenaline junkie? No problem at all. What difference does it make, come the end of the day? I'm achieving, I am actually achieving conservation on a greater level than anyone thought possible.'

Terri: 'I think his spirit and what he stood for needs to carry on forever.' The staff at Australia Zoo will carry his legacy forward.

Steve's dad would have been horrified at the thought that he encouraged him to risk his life. Ever since that first encounter with a Brown snake Bob did everything he could to teach his son about the dangers of wildlife. Nevertheless, he, too, accepted that there were risks in the life they both led.

'Over the years, Steve and I have had a lot of adventures together and there have been many occasions when anything could have gone wrong,' Bob stated after his son's death. But, he continued, 'Steve knew the risks involved with the type of work he was doing and he wouldn't have wanted it any other way.'

Chapter 8

Legacy

The thing that would have made Steve happiest after his death was the immediate surge in donations to the Wildlife Warriors charity. Michael Hornby, the director of Wildlife Warriors Worldwide, said that immediately following the tragedy they were receiving, on average, 55 donations every TEN minutes. It was only after Steve's death that the full extent of his charity work emerged and people realised how much difference he had made to conservation issues.

The thing that would have made him unhappiest, however, was the so-called revenge attacks on stingrays. He always said that, if he got bitten or stung, it was his fault and his fault alone. 'I would never blame an animal if it bit me, that is for sure,' he said to one interviewer, 'because I'm at fault, not them.'

In his interview with Andrew Denton he admitted that he'd often been scared by animals, but he said that people were worse.

'Unfortunately, in my line of work, I have to deal in some really heavy-duty places,' he said. 'People factor does actually scare the living daylights out of me, and I've seen some pretty awful, icky sort of things going on.'

Despite the overwhelmingly positive response to his work this was borne out after the funeral as phoney websites were set up to con money out of fans and two women were arrested for selling bogus Steve Irwin charity stickers. John Stainton described their actions as despicable.

'The fact that people are cashing in, so to speak, on his legacy, trying to sell stuff like that for fund raising supposedly or even resale of the tickets for the memorial service, all of those things are really just not on and they're just not Australian,' he said.

Despite these setbacks the overwhelming response from people who'd worked with Steve Irwin was that his work should continue. Immediately after the tragedy John Stainton even promised that they would complete the TV series they'd been working on when he died.

'I intend to finish *Ocean's Deadliest* with Philippe's help,' he said. 'Eventually we'll get that film made… as a tribute to Steve's final documentary on earth.'

'It is definitely going to be very difficult to finish this show, not just for myself, but for the incredible crew,' admitted Philippe. Ironically, of course, Steve wasn't filming for *Ocean's Deadliest* when he was killed. He was filming what should have been soft, innocent pieces for his daughter Bindi's *Jungle Girl* show.

But, on the eve of the public memorial service, Bindi promised that she, too, would continue filming. She even said that she'd swim with stingrays in the same part of the ocean where her father had died.

Dr Leo Smith, an expert on venomous fish from New York, said that one small reason Steve Irwin's death was so sad was that 'the last thing you want is for the guy who says things are safe to be killed' so perhaps he'd have been reassured by the fact that the people closest to Steve still understood his message. Australia Zoo prides itself on a philosophy of 'conservation through exciting education' and Steve always believed that people could learn what not to do from him, as well as what they should do.

Despite all the criticism he did believe in respect for nature. The thing that scared him most was that, with so many species disappearing, Bindi's generation might not get a chance to enjoy it. That's why he put so much effort into his wildlife charity. As Michael Hornby put it, 'there are many worthwhile organisations out there, but at end of the day, if our planet's not safe, you know, everything else is irrelevant.'

Steve with pure-bred Sumatran tiger cubs, which were part of Australia Zoo's breeding programme for endangered species.

In His Own Words

On his most feared creature...

'For some reason parrots have to bite me. That's their job. I don't know why that is. They've nearly torn my nose off. I've had some really bad parrot bites.'

On Hollywood...

'Crikey, mate. You're far safer dealing with crocodiles and Western Diamondback rattlesnakes than the executives and the producers and all those sharks in the big MGM building.'

On his approach to wildlife...

'I get called an adrenaline junkie every other minute, and I'm just fine with that.'

On his life...

'I have no fear of losing my life – if I have to save a koala or a crocodile or a kangaroo or a snake, mate, I will save it.'

On conservation...

'Every cent we earn from Crocodile Hunter goes straight back into conservation. Every single cent.'

On the future of the planet...

'I am optimistic globally. So many scientists are working frantically on the reparation of our planet.'

On his philosophy...

'We don't own the planet Earth, we belong to it.'

On education...

'I believe that education is all about being excited about something. Seeing passion and enthusiasm helps push an educational message.'

On farming...

'I sincerely believe that there's room for cutting down trees for forestry and grazing, so as we all get to eat. Everyone has to compromise.'

On his TV persona...

'My belief is that what comes across on the television is a capture of my enthusiasm and my passion for wildlife.'

On fear...

'Fear helps me from making mistakes, but I make lot of mistakes.'

On his presenting style...

'When I talk to the camera, mate, it's not like I'm talking to the camera, I'm talking to you because I want to whip you around and plunk you right there with me.'

On the difference between Hollywood and Beerwah...

'Where I live if someone gives you a hug it's from the heart.'

On Australia...

'I'm a proud Australian, a very, very proud Australian.'

On saving lives...

'I've probably saved thousands of peoples' lives with my educational message on snake bites.'

On American TV...

'No matter where you go and what you do in America, you turn the telly on and you're confronted with violence.'

On crocodiles...

'There are 23 species of crocodile. Seventeen of those species are rare or endangered. They're on the way out, no matter what anyone does or says, you know.'

On kangaroos...

'I think it's an absolute disaster that Australia, the government, allowed kangaroo culling.'

On King Kong...

'It hurt my feelings when they killed King Kong.'

On how his life has and hasn't changed...

'What happens is the cameras follow me around and capture exactly what I've been doing since I was a boy. Only now we have a team of, you know, like 73 of us, and it's gone beyond that.'

To find out more about Steve Irwin's charity work, or to make a donation, go to www.wildlifewarriors.org.au/